Making Magnificent Machines

Machines

Fun with Math, Science, and Engineering

Carol McBride

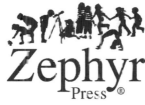

Zephyr
Press ®

REACHING THEIR HIGHEST POTENTIAL

Tucson, Arizona

Making Magnificent Machines
Fun with Math, Science, and Engineering

Grades: K through 8

© 2000 by Zephyr Press
Printed in the United States of America

ISBN 1-56976-102-7

Editing: Veronica Durie and Stacey Shropshire
Cover design: Daniel Miedaner
Design and production: Daniel Miedaner
Author photograph: Cassie McBride Gonzales

Zephyr Press
P.O. Box 66006
Tucson, AZ 85728-6006
1-800-232-2187
http://www.zephyrpress.com

Library of Congress Cataloging-in-Publication Data
McBride, Carol, 1955-
    Making magnificent machines : fun with math, science, and
engineering / Carol McBride.
        p.   cm.
    Summary: Provides instructions for building and using seventeen
mechanical projects, including an airplane, catapult, bobbing dog,
and submarine.
    ISBN 1-56976-102-7
    1. Machine design Juvenile literature.   [1. Machinery.]
I. Title.
TJ147M35   1999
62.8'15—dc21   99-34584

To my family,
Francisco Gonzales,
Misa Gonzales, and
Cassie Gonzales,
for all their brain power

Contents

Introduction

Making Magnificent Machines offers great projects that will get your students interested in learning math, engineering, and science concepts. The projects will pique students' interest, then lead them to discover the various principles that make machines work. Instead of simply memorizing such abstract concepts as kinetic and potential energy, for example, students have concrete experiences with these concepts that will forever embed them in their brains.

Helping students build these machines is an exciting learning process for you, as well. You'll be applying the same principles as the students, and you may find some untapped talent you never knew you had before. You'll be having fun with your students, so they'll know that you think learning is fun and that you value learning yourself.

Perhaps most important, though, you may discover strengths in your students that you wouldn't have otherwise known existed. Sometimes the children who are least successful on paper-and-pencil tests are those who really shine when asked to do something with their hands. You may find that the students you thought were simply "not getting it" are the ones who understand most intuitively how to apply the very concepts you are teaching. You can use this avenue to help such children do better on written tests, as well.

I'm always amazed at the unexpected ways in which children in my classes add to and improve my projects. I have learned never to interfere with the kids' designs of the wings on the airplane and launcher, for example. Sometimes the large clunky wings that I think will crash and burn carry the airplane in a graceful glide across the room much farther than the more streamlined designs. The children's persistence and the effectiveness of their own designs always surprise me.

Building the projects also allows you and your students to use many skills that simply reading a text does not allow. Students learn the value of high-quality, precise work. The mouse project works wonderfully only if all the parts have been measured precisely and adjusted accurately. The airplanes will fly only if the wings are designed well, if the body and wings achieve a balance of sorts, if they are constructed out of the right materials, and if the pieces are cut correctly.

Students also learn how to work with others. They may need help for some steps, and they may find that they have to put all their heads together to figure out why their machine doesn't work.

They solve problems in creative ways. They learn to experiment and change perspective to see if they can help something work even better. Sometimes they change the shape of the nose of the airplane, or they might add weight to it to see if it flies better. They also might try turning it upside down to fly it.

Math Skills

✦ Measuring enhances addition, subtraction, multiplication, and division skills.

✦ Students understand ratios by adjusting the size of one element in relation to the size of another.

✦ Cutting correct angles and aligning materials and tools correctly are applied geometry at its best.

Science Skills

✦ Students understand potential and kinetic energy; potential energy is the stretched rubber band, for example, that becomes kinetic energy when it is released to unwind.

✦ Students understand structural integrity. Adding supports where needed, for example, ensures that a machine will last longer.

✦ Students learn the properties of various materials. Plastic is waterproof; cardboard isn't. Corrugated cardboard tends to have more strength and less flexibility than cardboard that isn't corrugated. If they use masking tape for a boat, the boat won't last as long as if they use the sturdier, waterproof duct tape. And if they need to replace batteries, duct tape will make that task much more difficult.

✦ I'm still learning about properties and materials, too. The first time I made the hydro rocket with a large group, we used paper towel tubes for the rocket. After about the tenth time we shot off our rockets, the cardboard was soggy and falling apart, even though we had used a plastic lid as the base. We all quickly exchanged the tubes for some plastic film containers, which drastically improved our results.

Safety

I cannot stress strongly enough that most of these projects require close adult supervision. Students will often be cutting with tools much sharper and stronger than scissors. There can also be harmless, mild sparks from the projects that require batteries and electrical connections. As much as possible, you want students to be able to do all the steps themselves, but if you have any questions about whether they are capable of doing something that is potentially harmful, always always err on the side of safety.

The most important aspect of this book is that students love these projects. They work on them willingly and with great enthusiasm. I've had students talk their parents into changing vacation days around so that they will not miss my class. They also feel the joy of ownership that only creation can provide. My husband once taught the boat project in a summer program. The week after they had completed the boats and were working on another machine, one student moaned to my husband, "The boat I made last week fell apart!" His mom told my husband, "He played with it for six hours in the bathtub. He looked like a prune and the boat finally gave up!"

The bat wings always create excitement in the classroom. It doesn't matter that the children know what is going to pop out of their hand-made envelopes; everyone still jumps and screams. The last time we made bat wings in my class, one boy wound the rubber band so tightly that when he opened the envelope, the wings shot high over his shoulder. A bit shaken, he said, "I'm outta here!" but he was laughing too hard to move.

More Books with Fun Machines

Hann, Judith. 1991. *How Science Works.* New York: Reader's Digest Association.

Macauley, David. 1988. *The Way Things Work.* Boston: Houghton Mifflin.

Maganzini, Christy. 1997. *Cool Math.* New York: Price Stern Sloan.

Maynard, Christopher. 1993. *I Wonder Why Planes Have Wings.* New York: Kingfisher.

Nye, Bill. 1995. *Bill Nye the Science Guy's Consider the Following: A Way Cool Set of Science Questions, Answers, and Ideas to Ponder.* New York: Disney Press.

Taylor, Charles, and Stephen Pople. 1995. *The Oxford Children's Book of Science.* Oxford, N.Y.: Oxford University Press.

Walpole, Brenda. 1987. *Fun with Science Movement.* New York: Warwick Press.

White, David. 1989. *The Great Book of Submarines.* Vero Beach, Fla.: Rourke Enterprises.

Whittle, Fran, and Sarah Lawrence. 1998. *Simple Machines.* Austin, Tex.: Steck-Vaughn.

Wyler, Rose. 1986. *Science Fun with Toy Boats and Planes.* New York: Julian Messner.

Connections to Curriculum

W ithin the pages of this book, you will find step-by-step instructions for the construction of whimsical moving machines. Most of the activities explore the mechanics of motion, drawing on key concepts and standards for learning outlined in the *National Science Educational Standards*. Each project provides avenues for students to explore performance possibilities of the machines by varying materials or dimensions while maintaining consistency in the construction process.

The necessary inclusion of measurement, geometric and spatial sense, and opportunities for computation provides means to address the *National Council of Teachers of Mathematics Standards*.

Following is a list of science standards, mathematics standards, and key concepts addressed within this book. For each activity and each concept or standard listed, the complexity of the exploration will vary according to age, cognitive strength, and interest.

Science as Inquiry

Science as inquiry is a natural piece or extension of each project in this book. The NSES offer this method:

> *Science as Inquiry is basic to science education and a controlling principle in the ultimate organization and selection of student activities. Students in all grade levels and in every domain of science should have the opportunity to think and act in ways associated with inquiry such as asking questions, planning and conducting investigations, using appropriate tools and techniques to gather data, and thinking critically and logically about relationships between evidence and explanation, constructing and analyzing alternative explanations, and communicating scientific arguments. (NSES document, 1996)*

Physical Science

The construction projects in this book address a number of key physical science concepts as well as several content standards listed in the NSES Physical Science category and the NCTM curriculum standards for mathematics.

Key Concepts

potential energy

kinetic energy

electrical energy

inclined plane

fulcrum

lever

pulley

weights and balances

characteristics of moving objects

principles of flight

action and reaction

NSES Content Standards

properties of objects and materials

position and motion of objects

motions and forces

electricity

transfer of energy

NCTM Curriculum Standards

mathematical connections

estimation

concepts of whole number operations

whole number computation

geometry and spatial sense

measurement

fractions and decimals

patterns and relationships

AIRPLANES AND LAUNCHERS

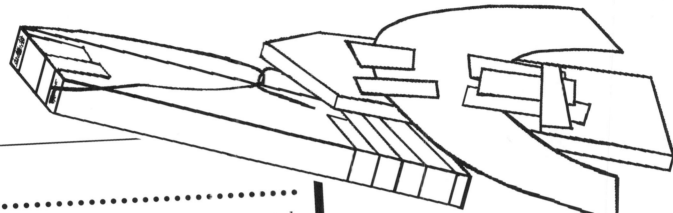

SUPPLIES

- one sturdy, ¹/₈- to ¹/₄-inch-thick piece corrugated cardboard or foam core for the airplane body

- one cereal box, one paper plate, or one polystyrene grocery tray washed with soap and water before using for wings

- low-temperature mini-glue sticks

- masking tape

- one steel paper clip

- one size 18 rubber band for the launcher

- one approximately 2-by-12-by-¹/₂-inch piece of wood or a wooden ruler to work as a launcher

- paint

TOOLS

- high-quality adult craft scissors with a spring in the handle

- marker or pencil

- low-temperature, mini-glue gun

- paintbrush

1

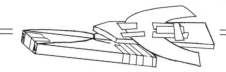

INSTRUCTIONS

Step 1

For the airplane body, with the scissors **cut** a 1½- to 2-inch-wide strip about 7 to 9 inches long out of corrugated cardboard, foam core, or any similar strong material (see diagram 1).

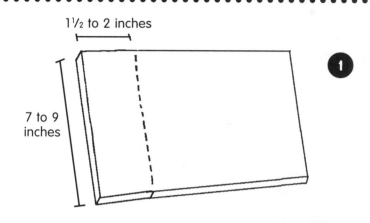

1½ to 2 inches

7 to 9 inches

1

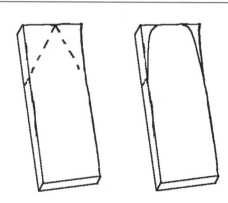

2a

Step 2

Draw a pointed or rounded tip on one end of the airplane body (see diagram 2a). **Cut** carefully along the line (see diagram 2b).

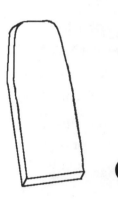

2b

Step 3

Draw your wings onto one of a variety of household materials (see diagram 3). My favorite is polystyrene grocery trays used to package meat, fruit, and vegetables. They are strong, lightweight, and easy to cut. Cereal boxes or paper plates work great, too. Be creative. Pick a shape you think will help your airplane glide well. Use scissors to **cut** out your wings.

3

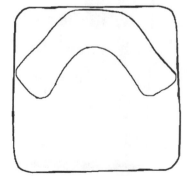

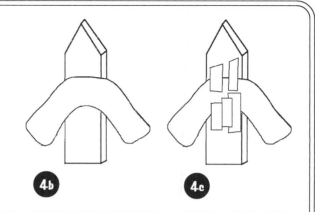

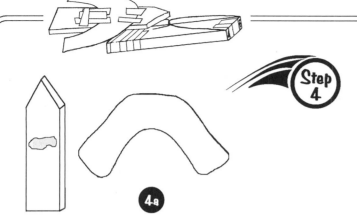

Step 4

Apply a little bit of glue from the glue gun to the top of the airplane body (see diagram 4a). **Press** the wings into the glue (see diagram 4b). **Tape** the wings with masking tape (see diagram 4c).

4a

4b

4c

Step 5

Tape crosswise over your original tape to prevent it from pulling loose (see diagram 5).

5

Note

Do not put the wings on the bottom of your airplane.

6

Step 6

Carefully **unroll** the paper clip until there is a hook at one end and the rest of it is straight (see diagram 6).

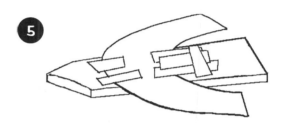

Step 7

With the glue gun, **run** a line of glue along the bottom of the airplane body. Carefully **set** the straight edge of the paper clip, hook side up, in the warm, not hot, sticky glue (see diagram 7). **Squeeze** a little more glue on top of the paper clip.

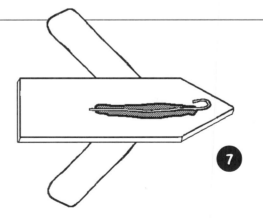

7

Step 8

Place tape crosswise along the entire straight edge of the paper clip and the warm glue (see diagram 8). The glue and tape will keep the paper clip securely attached to the airplane body.

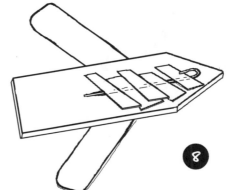

8

Warning
Do not point the airplane at anyone while launching.

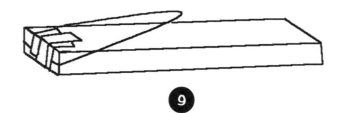

9

Step 9

To make the launcher, **tape** a rubber band securely to the end of the stick or ruler (see diagram 9). *Note: Do not use too much tape* because you will have to replace the rubber band every once in a while when it breaks.

Step 10

If the wood of your launcher is rough or splintery, **wrap** tape around the handle to avoid splinters (see diagram 10).

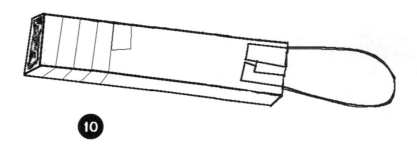

10

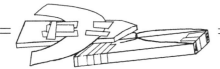

Step 11

Grip the handle of the launcher with one hand. With your other hand, **hook** the paper clip onto the rubber band (see diagram 11). **Pull** back as far as you can, **point** the launcher and the airplane up toward the sky, and **let go**.

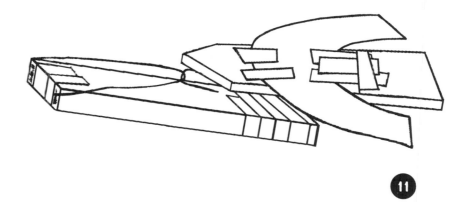

11

Step 12

Add structural details and decorations to the top of your airplane (see diagram 12). Experiment. **Add** fins. **Test fly** it before and after adding parts to see which additions work best. Sometimes I tape a penny to the front end of the airplane. Or I might use the glue gun and tape to attach a broken crayon to the top of the airplane at the nose to increase its weight. These steps can make it fly faster and straighter.

Note

Anything on the bottom of the airplane besides the paper clip will interfere with the airplane launching.

Step 13

Paint the airplane.

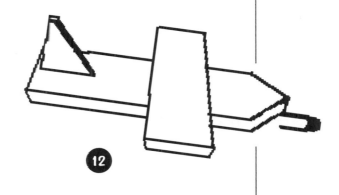

12

MINIATURE AIRPLANE AND LAUNCHER

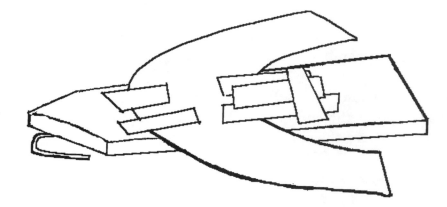

SUPPLIES

- ✦ one size 18 or smaller rubber band
- ✦ one tongue depressor for launcher
- ✦ masking tape
- ✦ cardboard scraps or foam core scraps for the airplane body
- ✦ cereal box scraps for wings
- ✦ one small steel paper clip
- ✦ low-temperature mini-glue sticks
- ✦ paint

TOOLS

- ★ marker or pencil
- ★ high-quality adult craft scissors with a spring in the handle
- ★ heavy-duty diagonal cutting pliers to cut the paper clip in half
- ★ low-temperature glue gun
- ★ paintbrush

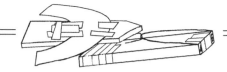

INSTRUCTIONS

Step 1

To make the miniature launcher, **tape** the rubber band to the bottom of the end of a tongue depressor with a length of tape extending beyond the depressor (see diagram 1a). **Fold** the tape extension tightly around the rubber band and **attach** it to the bottom of the tongue depressor (see diagram 1b).

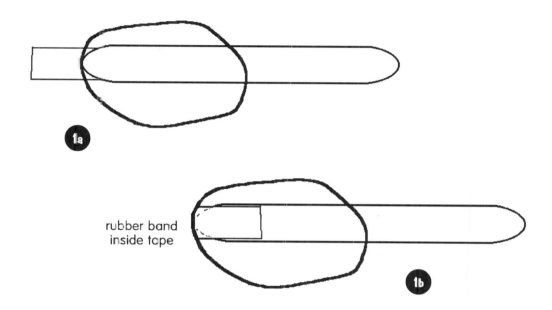

1a

rubber band inside tape

1b

Step 2

To make the miniature airplane, draw and cut out an airplane body 3 to 6 inches long using scraps from the large airplane. **Draw** and **cut out** wings, following directions for large airplane.

Step 3

Unroll the paper clip until there is one hook left in it. Use the strong pliers to cut the paper clip in half.

Step 4

Attach the half with the hook to the airplane, hook side up, with the glue gun and masking tape.

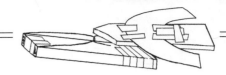

Step 5

Test fly it and **add** personal touches; **paint** it (see diagram 5).

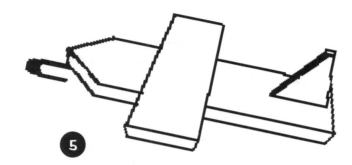

5

Warning

Do not point the airplane at anyone while launching.

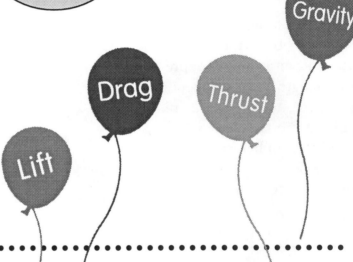

Gravity

Drag

Thrust

Lift

ELEMENTS THAT AFFECT FLIGHT

Four things affect the way your airplane flies through the air: *gravity, thrust, lift,* and *drag.* Gravity is the force caused by the rotation of the planet that wants to pull your airplane to the ground. The thrust comes from your launching it with the rubber band attached to a stick. Lift occurs when air flows under the flat surfaces of the airplane, creating a greater force than what gravity has on it. The airplane will fly higher and longer if you design the wings longer and wider to create a larger flat surface

for the air to affect. A horseshoe shape also works well. Why? Drag occurs when elements of the airplane, such as its shape and thickness, cause the air to work in opposition to the elements that lift it. The airplane slows. You can help it fly faster by streamlining it, that is, by not adding elements that may catch the air, keeping it from going freely over and under the airplane. By understanding these elements, you can design your airplane to soar higher, longer, and farther.

BAT WINGS

Supplies

- ✦ one large steel paper clip
- ✦ one small piece of corrugated cardboard or foam core
- ✦ markers
- ✦ two size 16 or 18 rubber bands
- ✦ one handmade envelope (see page 11) or legal size envelope

Tools

- ★ needle-nose pliers
- ★ high-quality adult craft scissors with a spring in the handle
- ★ hole punch

Instructions

 **Step 1** Carefully **unroll** (don't twist) the paper clip (see diagram 1a) until it looks like an *L* (see diagram 1b).

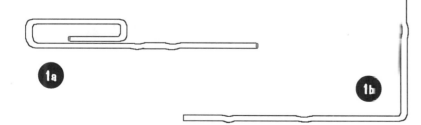

1a

1b

 **Step 2** Use the needle-nose pliers to **twist** the ends of the paper clip inward into loops around the pliers (see diagram 2).

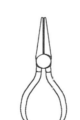

needle-nose pliers

2

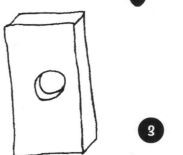

Step 3 **Cut** a ³/₄-by-1¹/₄-inch rectangle of cardboard or foam core. With the hole punch, **punch** a hole in the middle (see diagram 3). You may need an adult to help you with this step. **Color** the rectangle with markers.

3

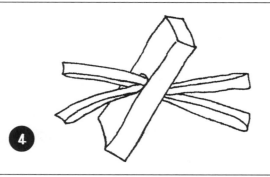

4

Insert the two rubber bands into the hole (see diagram 4). **Step 4**

Step 5 **Separate** the rubber bands. **Pull** the ends of each rubber band to the side like butterfly wings (see diagram 5).

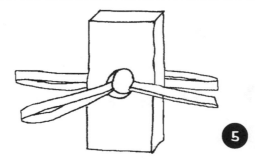

5

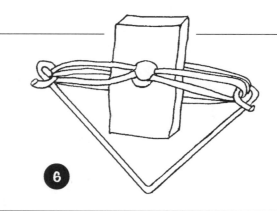

Attach the two loops of each rubber band to one loop of the bent paper clip (see diagram 6). Test the apparatus by **twisting** the rectangle around to wind up the rubber bands. **Let go** of the cardboard. It should unwind easily. **Step 6**

6

 **Wind up** the bat wings again, then place the device in the envelope. **Hold** the outside of the envelope so that you are also holding the bat wings still. **Hand** the envelope to someone with the open end of the envelope toward you; the person will have to clasp the envelope right at the bat wings. If she has a good grip on the bat wings inside the envelope, then the wings will not unwind *until she looks inside.*

ENVELOPE

Supplies

+ one 8½-by-11 inch sheet of copier paper

+ staples or masking tape

+ markers, crayons, or other items to decorate the envelope

Tools

★ stapler, if not using masking tape

Instructions

 The lightweight paper makes lots of noise and allows the bat wings to unwind easily. **Fold** the paper crosswise not quite in half; allow about an inch to extend above the edge of the top fold (see diagram 1). This extension is the envelope flap.

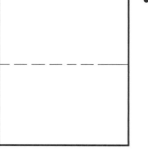

11

 **Staple** or **tape** both sides of the envelope closed (see diagram 2).

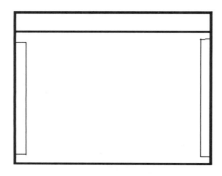

②

 **Decorate** the envelope and **name** it something that sounds scary: alligator lips, baby spiders, dinosaur eggs, bat wings, spider eggs (see diagram 3).

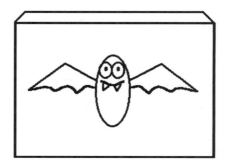

③

Troubleshooting

- If the rectangle doesn't unwind easily, it may be too big; trim its edges.

Bat Wing Energy

The energy created by the rubber band unwinding causes the cardboard rectangle to move like a paddle. The paddle motion throws the bat wings out of the envelope. Experiment: What happens if you wind the rubber bands tightly? Loosely?

The rectangle shape of the cardboard or foam core causes the bat wings to paddle out of the envelope. If you do not want them to pop out, then you can cut your cardboard about 1 inch square. It will just make noise.

BOATS

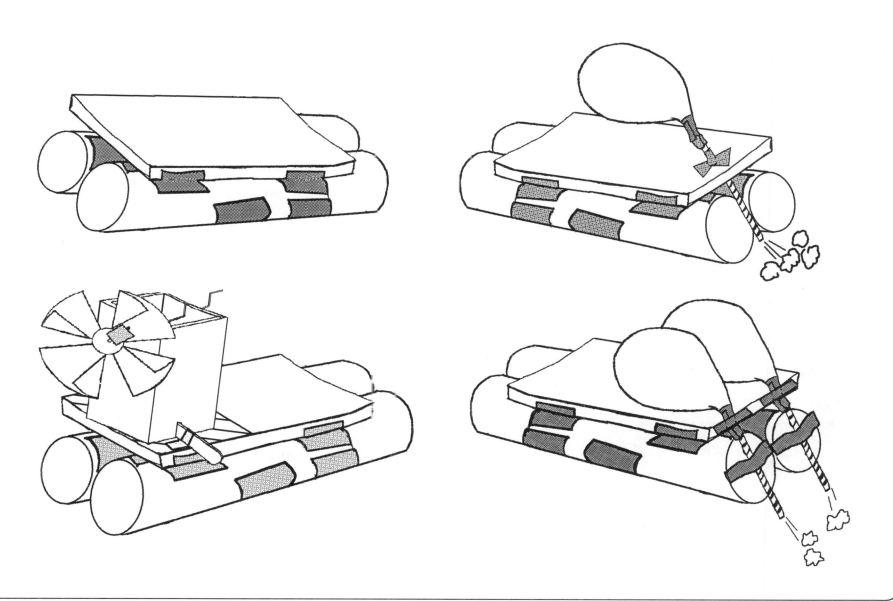

BASIC BOAT

This boat is used as a base for all the other boats in this chapter

SUPPLIES

- four clean, dry, 12-ounce aluminum cans
- duct tape
- one large piece corrugated cardboard or foam core for the boat deck
- items to decorate boat such as egg cartons, toilet paper and paper towel tubes, plastic containers
- low-temperature mini-glue sticks
- paint if painting boat

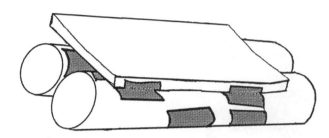

TOOLS

- high-quality adult craft scissors with a spring in the handle
- low-temperature mini-glue gun
- paintbrush if painting boat

INSTRUCTIONS

 **Step 1**

Remove the pop-tops from the aluminum cans (see diagram 1).

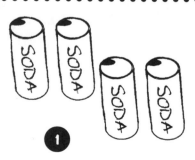

1

 **Step 2**

Place two cans together top to top, openings together. This step keeps water from getting into the cans. **Repeat** with other two cans (see diagram 2) .

 **2**

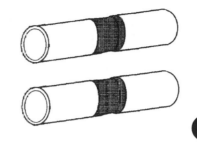

Make sure there aren't any gaps in your tape. The outside of duct tape is waterproof, but if there are gaps, water can weaken the tape's glue against the cans.

Step 3 Cut duct tape and hang it off of your worktable so you can pick the pieces up easily. Hold the cans together. **Duct-tape** the cans together (see diagram 3).

3

Do not overtape!

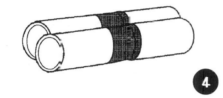

4

Step 4 **Duct-tape** the four cans together, side by side (see diagram 4), placing the tape anywhere along the length of the cans.

Step 5 Cut a 7-by-10-inch piece of cardboard or foam core. **Duct-tape** the piece of cardboard or foam core to the top of the cans to form the boat deck (see diagram 5). The boat is buoyant—you may make a larger deck if you want. You can also add more cans to create a bigger floating device.

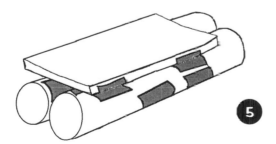

5

Step 6 If you are not making a balloon or propeller boat, **paint** and **decorate** the boat. **Glue** the decorations to the boat with the glue gun. Decorate both sides evenly or the boat will tip over. You might want to build the miniature airplane and launcher on page 6 and attach the launcher to the boat to make an aircraft carrier.

PROPELLER BOAT

SUPPLIES

- one basic boat (see page 14)
- marker or pencil
- one large piece corrugated cardboard or foam core for propeller box
- masking tape
- one large steel paper clip for the crank
- one size 18 rubber band
- two Popsicle or craft sticks
- one large heavy-duty paper plate or some kind of cardboard such as that used in cereal boxes for the propeller
- low-temperature mini-glue sticks
- paint

TOOLS

- high-quality adult craft scissors with a spring in the handle
- ruler
- X-acto knife
- needle-nose pliers
- pen
- low-temperature mini-glue gun
- paintbrush

INSTRUCTIONS

Step 1

About 5 inches from the back of the boat, with a pencil, **draw** a line across the deck (see diagram 1). This is where the propeller will be placed.

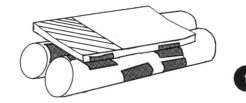

1

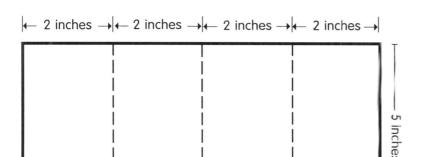

|← 2 inches →|← 2 inches →|← 2 inches →|← 2 inches →|

5 inches

2

Step 2

Cut a 5-by-8-inch piece of cardboard or foam core to make a box for the propeller. Use a ruler to **measure** and **draw** three crosswise lines 2 inches apart (see diagram 2). Ask an adult to **score** the dotted lines with an X-acto knife to make it easier to fold.

Step 3

Fold the cardboard to make a topless box (see diagram 3). **Tape** the opening together with masking tape. **Reinforce** the box with masking tape on all the folds if needed.

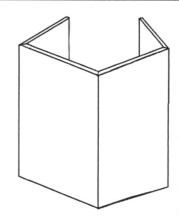

3

BOATS

Step 4

Draw two lines about ¹/₂ inch long on top of two sides opposite each other (see diagram 4). **Cut** along the lines. **Repeat** on the bottom of the two sides not already cut.

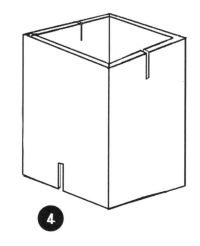

4

Unroll the paper clip, leaving one end pointing up (see diagram 5). This end will hold the fan.

Step 5

5

Step 6

With the needle-nose pliers, **bend** the end of the paper clip opposite the bent end up one inch, at a 90-degree angle (see diagram 6a). Then **grab** the bent end about halfway up, about ¹/₂ inch, and **bend** that section out (see diagram 6b). Be very careful not to bend too much up, as the paper clip must reach across the box you made even after you make the crankshaft in the next step. This side is your crank handle.

needle-nose pliers

Step 7

With the needle-nose pliers, **grip** the paper clip about ¹/₄ inch off center of the straight section (see diagram 7). **Wrap** the wire around the pliers to form a loop that is centered on the straight section of the paper clip. The rubber band will go through this crankshaft. Test to be sure that the paper clip reaches across the box.

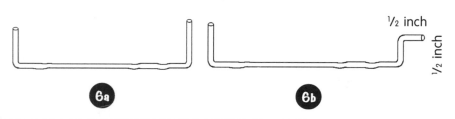

¹/₂ inch

¹/₂ inch

6a   **6b**

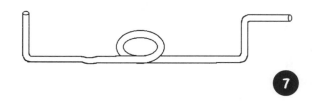

7

Insert the rubber band into the loop you made in step 7 (see diagram 8a). **Insert** one end of the rubber band into the other end of the rubber band (see diagram 8b). **Pull** until snug.

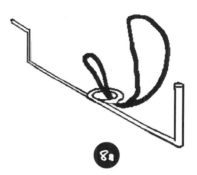

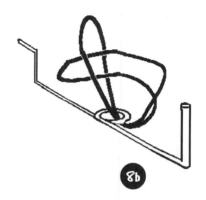

Very gently so that you do not bend or warp the paper clip, **push** the crank into the slits at the top of the box (see diagram 9). The crank should fit snugly, so be patient to work it in rather than making the cuts larger.

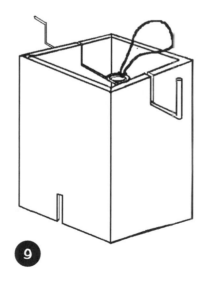

Pull the rubber band down through the box and **insert** a Popsicle or craft stick through the bottom loop (see diagram 10a). **Turn** the stick to align with the two cuts in the bottom of the box. **Insert** the stick into the cuts (see diagram 10b, page 20). The rubber band should be stretched tight, creating tension.

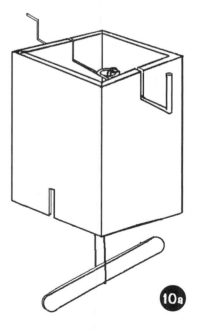

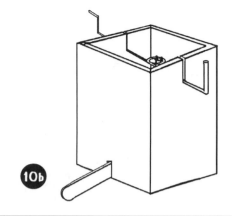

10b

Step 11

Hold on to the crank side of the paper clip and **turn** it, winding up the rubber band. **Let go** and **allow** the rubber band to unwind as the paper clip spins. It should unwind very quickly.

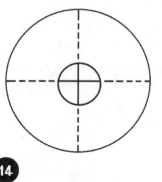

Warning
Get your fingers out of the way of the handle as soon as you let go of it.

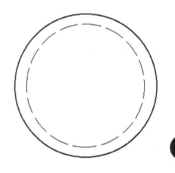

12

To make the propeller, **cut** a 5- to 9-inch circle from the center of a heavy-duty paper plate or out of a cereal box (see diagram 12). The larger propeller will work better because it can push more air.

Step 12

Step 13

Draw a giant plus sign on your paper plate circle, with the intersection in the very center of the circle (see diagram 13). Draw a 2-inch circle around the intersection (see diagram 13).

13

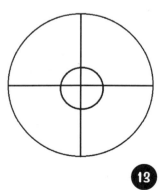

Step 14

Cut along the lines up to the outer edge of the circle (see diagram 14). **Do not cut inside the circle.**

14

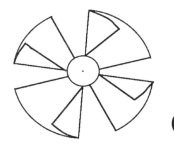

right-handed propeller

Step 15

Roll or fold up one side of each propeller blade according to whether you are right or left handed (see diagram 15). The propeller blades must be folded so they will work according to the direction the crank shaft is unwinding. Because a right-handed person will wind the crankshaft in the opposite direction than a left-handed person will, the blades must be folded differently for left- and right-handed people.

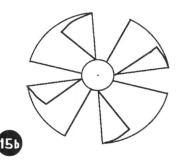

left-handed propeller

Step 16

With a pen, **poke** a hole just large enough to fit over the end of the paper clip into the middle of the propeller. **Place** the propeller on the end of the paper clip opposite the crankshaft, moving it around the bend (see diagram 16). **Tape** the wire snugly to the propeller. If it is wobbly, with the glue gun **place** a small glob of glue between the propeller and the paper clip. **Hold** it straight until it dries.

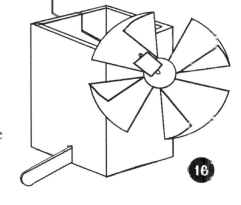

Step 17

Place the box on the boat deck, as close to the back edge of the boat as possible (see diagram 17). **Tape** both sides of the craft stick to the deck. Do not use glue because you will need to replace the rubber band when it breaks. If the box is too loose, tape it down as well.

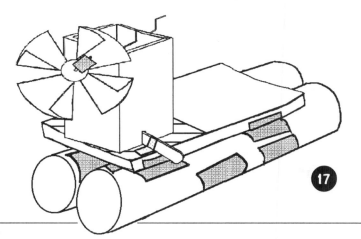

SCIENCE EXPERIMENT
• •

See if your boat works better with or without a sail. Using a ¼-inch dowel, attach a paper or cloth sail to your boat.

Step 18

Paint and **decorate** your propeller boat. Turn crank shaft, set boat in water, and watch it go!

BALLOON-POWERED BOAT

INSTRUCTIONS

 **Step 1** About 5 inches from the back of the boat, **draw** a line across the deck (see diagram 1). This is where the balloon will be placed.

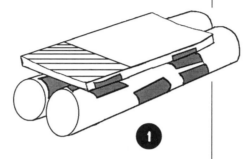

1

 **Step 2** **Blow** up the balloon a couple of times to stretch it out (see diagram 2). This will make it easier for you to blow up after you have connected it to the boat.

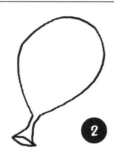

2

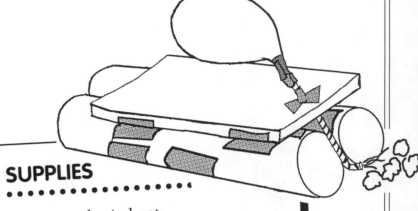

SUPPLIES

+ one basic boat
+ pencil or marker
+ one balloon
+ one plastic soda or coffee straw
+ duct tape
+ string

 **Step 3**

Insert a straw into the stem of the deflated balloon (see diagram 3).

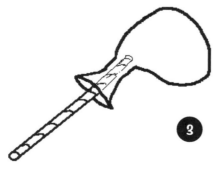

3

 **Step 4** **Push** the straw against one side of the inside of the balloon (see diagram 4).

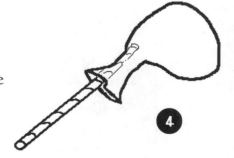

4

Step 5

Twist the stem of the balloon to wrap it tightly around the straw (see diagram 5).

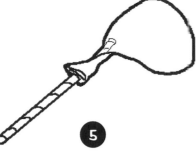

5

Step 6

Duct-tape around the stem of the balloon to hold the straw in place (see diagram 6).

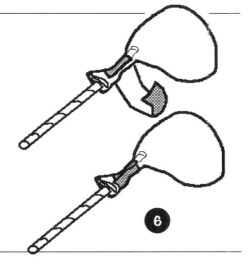

6

Step 7

Duct-tape lengthwise along the stem of the balloon, extending out onto the straw to fix the stem firmly to the straw (see diagram 7). The seal should be airtight.

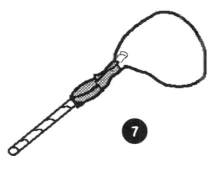

7

Step 8

Mark a place in the center of the deck about 1½ inches from the end from which you drew the line. Ask an adult to use scissors to poke a hole through the deck at the mark (see diagram 8). The straw should go between the cans when it is inserted into the hole.

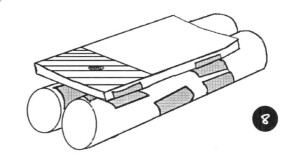

8

Step 9

Insert the end of the straw into the hole as far as it will go, until the stem of the balloon or the end of the tape rests on the deck (see diagram 9a). The straw should extend slightly beneath the aluminum cans so it will be in the water when you set the boat in the water. Duct-tape the straw securely to the deck (see diagram 9b).

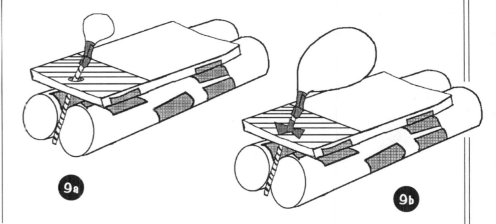

9a

9b

Step 10

Blow air through the straw to inflate the balloon (see diagram 10).

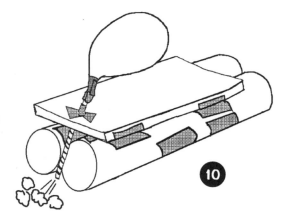

⑩

Step 11

Set the boat into water to ensure the straw's end is just below water level. Let it go to see how well the boat travels through water.

TROUBLESHOOTING

If the boat moves too quickly through the water, or it doesn't move very far, the air is moving too rapidly through the straw. Pinch the straw about ½ to 1 inch from the end of the deck and fold it up slightly (see diagram).

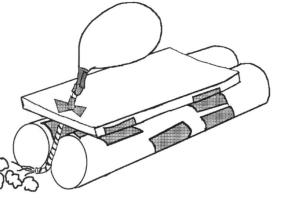

Step 12

Paint and **decorate** the boat. Tie a string to it so you can pull it back to you.

SCIENCE EXPERIMENTS

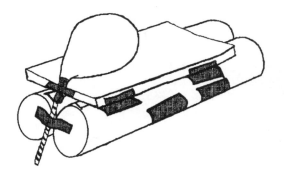

Try taping the straw to the back of the boat (see diagram). What happens to the boat when you tape the straw in the center? Slightly to the left? To the right?

Try a boat with two balloons (see diagram). What happens to the movement of your boat? Does it go straight? What if you fill up one balloon with more air than the other? What happens then?

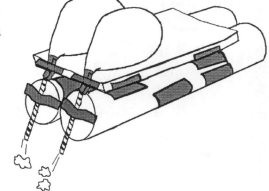

CANNON

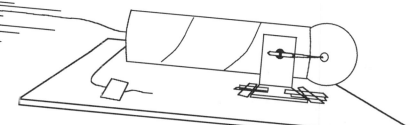

- white wood glue
- paint
- one paper towel tube
- one large piece of corrugated cardboard or foam core for cannon base
- one large piece of corrugated cardboard for the brackets
- masking tape
- one small plastic container, such as a pill bottle
- 2 to 3 feet of thin elastic string such as the kind used in children's play jewelry
- low-temperature mini-glue sticks
- one compact, 2-inch, strong, solid, polystyrene ball (not a porous ball) or two pieces of cardboard
- one size 18 rubber band
- two brass fasteners
- paper
- toilet paper tubes, yogurt cups, or other lightweight items for targets
- markers and pencils

TOOLS

- paintbrush
- high-quality adult craft scissors with a spring in the handle
- hole punch
- hammer and nail
- low-temperature mini-glue gun
- slim stick, such as a chopstick
- pipe cleaner

INSTRUCTIONS

CANNON

Step 1

If you want to paint the barrel of your cannon, it is easier to do it before you put it together (see diagram 1). **Pour** some white wood glue into the paint. **Mix** the paint and glue together. **Paint** the paper towel tube and **let dry**. The glue will make the tube stronger.

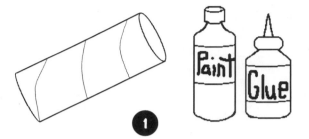

Cut an 8-by-14-inch piece of foam core or corrugated cardboard for the base (see diagram 2).

Step 2

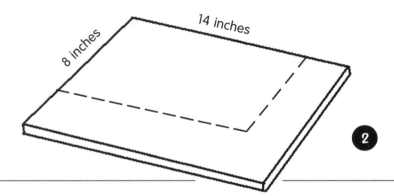

8 inches

14 inches

Step 3

Cut two 2-by-7-inch pieces of cardboard. The pieces do not have to be exactly the same size. With the hole punch, **punch** a hole in one end of each (see diagram 3).

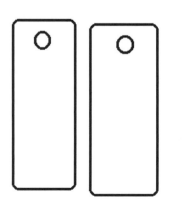

Fold the pieces of cardboard in half crosswise (see diagram 4), making sure the holes are the same distance from the folds. You can fold them over the edge of a table to make the creases straight.

Step 4

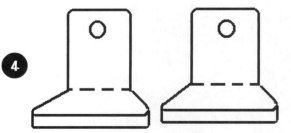

26

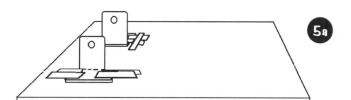

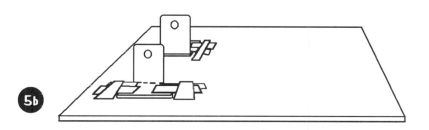

Step 5

Place the pieces of cardboard on one short end of the base, facing each other (see diagram 5a), approximately 2 inches apart (the width of the paper towel tube). Make sure the end with no hole is against the base. Tape the edges down, then tape across the tape so the pieces don't come loose when you shoot your cannon (see diagram 5b).

Step 6

Punch two holes in the paper towel tube across from each other, as far down the side of the tube as the hole punch will reach (see diagram 6). The farther down the holes, the less likely the tube is to tear.

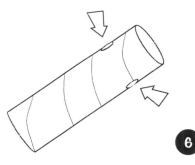

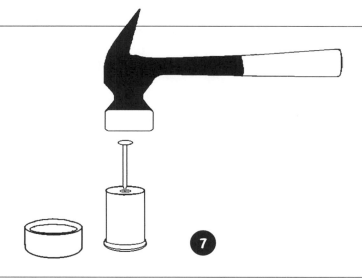

Step 7

Remove the lid from the plastic pill bottle and turn the bottle upside down. Hammer the nail through the bottom of the pill bottle to create a hole (see diagram 7). It doesn't matter if the hole is jagged or off center.

CANNON

27

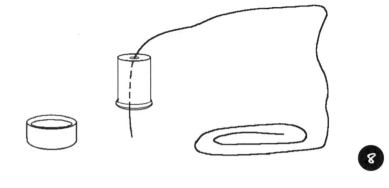

8

Step 8

Insert one end of the elastic string into the hole in the plastic pill bottle (see diagram 8). You can also use regular kite string or several rubber bands linked together instead of elastic string, but the elastic string works best.

Step 9

Leave an inch or so of string hanging out the top of the bottle and replace the lid (see diagram 9). Tighten the lid to capture the string and hold it snug.

9

Step 10

With the glue gun, **secure** the string to the bottle at the lid (see diagram 10). The string will not slide out of the bottle.

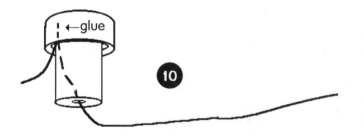

←glue

10

Note

If you do not have a plastic bottle, use a toilet paper tube. Cut the tube lengthwise, put the string through the center of the tube, run a stream of glue along the string to fasten it to the tube, then roll up the tube and glue it in place (see diagram).

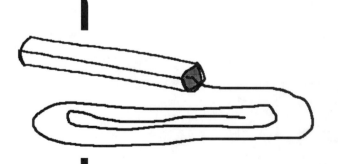

Step 11

There is usually a hole in one end of a polystyrene ball. **Insert** the slim stick into the hole and **push while twisting** to drill the hole all the way through the ball (see diagram 11).

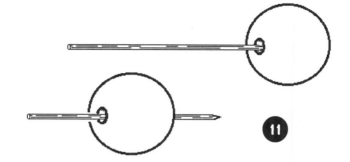

11

Step 12

Put the rubber band over one end of the pipe cleaner and **fold** the end over (see diagrams 12a and 12b). Twist the pipe cleaner tightly together so that the rubber band doesn't bulge (see diagram 12c).

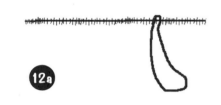

12a

12b

12c

Step 13

Insert the pipe cleaner through the hole in the polystyrene ball until it is almost all the way through. Leave the rubber band dangling outside the ball (see diagram 13).

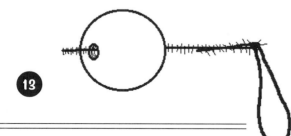

13

Note

If you don't have a good polystyrene ball try other things. For example, you can glue together two 2-by-3-inch pieces of heavy cardboard. Cut notches into each side to hold the rubber band in place and connect it to the cannon as you would the polystyrene ball (see diagram). Continue with the rest of the instructions.

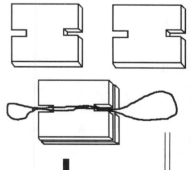

29

Step 14

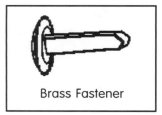

Brass Fastener

Keep the ball on top of the barrel of the cannon throughout the next two steps so you have room to stick your hand inside the paper towel tube. **Insert** a brass fastener into each hole from the inside of the paper towel tube. Open them slightly so they stay in. **Hook** the rubber band to one fastener (see diagram 14a). **Insert** the fastener through the hole in the cardboard that is attached to the base and open it (see diagram 14b). Tape the fastener in place (see diagram 14c).

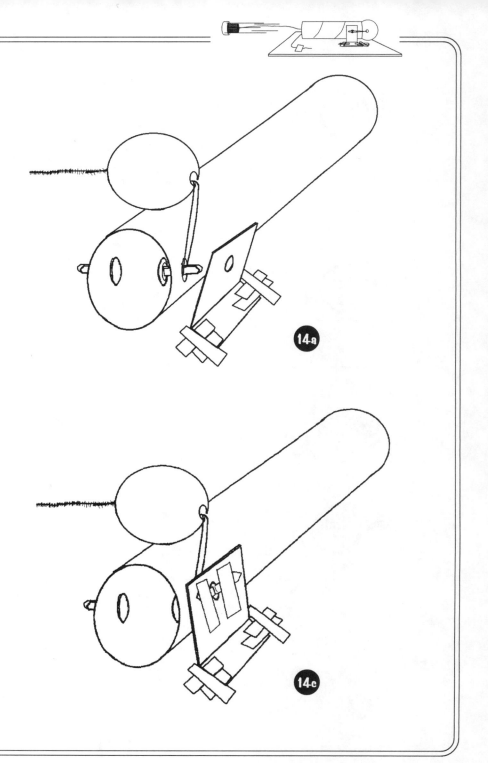

14a

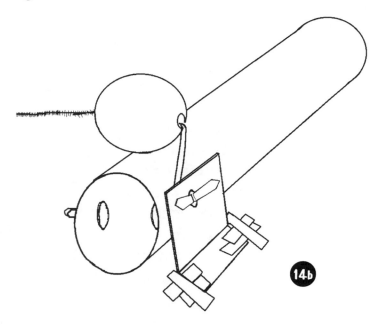

14b

14c

Step 15

Pull the pipe cleaner the rest of the way through the polystyrene ball and grab that end of the rubber band. **Remove** the pipe cleaner. **Connect** the rubber band to the free brass fastener, then **insert** the fastener through the other side. **Open** the fastener and **tape** it to the holder. The rubber band should connect to both fasteners with the polystyrene ball in the middle (see diagram 15).

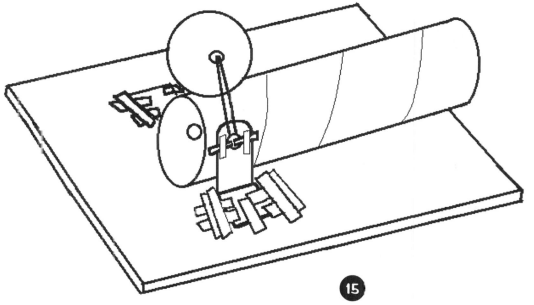

15

Step 16

Move the polystyrene ball to the back of the cannon (see diagram 16).

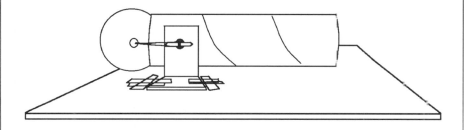

16

Step 17

Tape the free end of the elastic string to the base, with the pill bottle on the other end (see diagram 17).

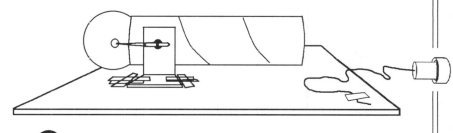

17

Step 18

Draw some targets on paper (see diagram 18a).
Cut them out and **glue** or **tape** them to something
lightweight such as toilet paper tubes or yogurt
containers (see diagram 18b). **Place** the targets
several inches in front of the cannon barrel.

18a

18b

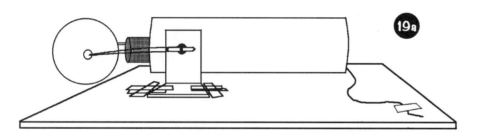

19a

Step 19

Put the bottle bottom
first into the front of the
cannon barrel. **Pull** back
the polystyrene ball and
allow the pill bottle to
slide halfway out of the
back of the barrel (see
diagram 19a). **Let go** of
the polystyrene ball and
let it hit the pill bottle.
It will make a *boom*
sound and thrust the
plastic pill bottle out of
the tube (see diagram
19b). The pill bottle will
knock over your target.

BOING   BOING

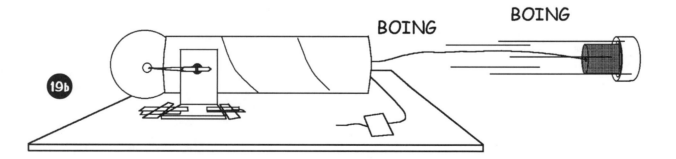

19b

TROUBLESHOOTING

The tube may tear around the holes with use. If yours tears, either cut the tube shorter and punch new holes, or turn the tube around and punch holes in the other end.

SCIENCE AND MATH EXPERIMENT

Calculate how fast your cannon shoots. With a partner, measure the distance between the front of the barrel and the target. One person fires the cannon while another person times how long it takes for the bottle to hit the target. The second person can either use a stopwatch or count "one thousand one, one thousand 2, . . ." Calculate the velocity (v) (or the speed over distance) by dividing the distance (d) by the time (t) it takes to travel that distance. The equation for this calculation is $v = d/t$.

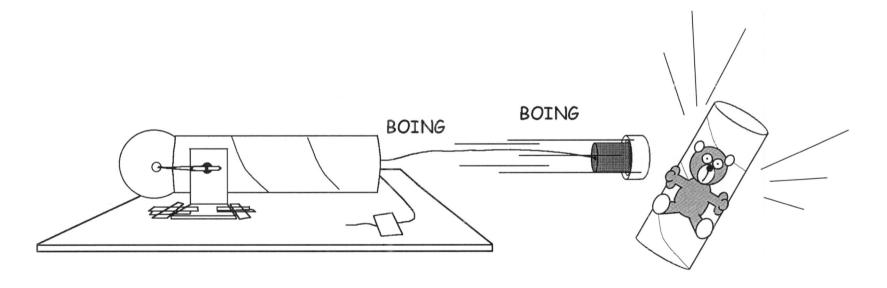

BOING   BOING

THREE-WHEELED MOTOR CAR

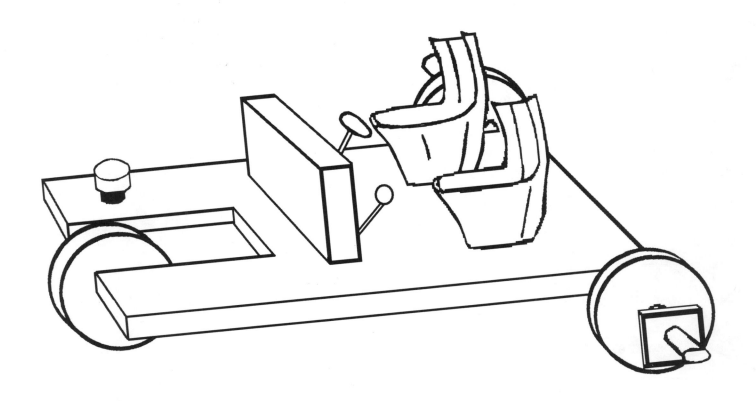

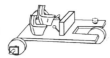

SUPPLIES

- one piece ¼-inch corrugated cardboard or foam core for the frame, and for separators and hubcaps
- marker or pencil
- one ¼-inch dowel or one chopstick for the axle
- masking tape
- one smooth swimming pool noodle for tires (noodles with ridges will cause the tires to drag)
- low-temperature mini-glue sticks
- thin, flexible toilet paper tube or half of a thin paper towel tube for the battery pack (some may be too thick and stiff to work with)
- two AA batteries
- one cereal box or other lightweight cardboard
- 22-gauge copper wire for two spring connectors
- one plastic cap from a sport water bottle
- one 1.5- to 3-volt DC, single-speed motor purchased from an electronics store (see diagram)
- one push on, push off switch from an electronics store (see diagram)
- one ⅞- to 1-inch dowel or a small chunk of wood
- 22-gauge coated copper wire
- paint
- egg carton

TOOLS

- high-quality adult craft scissors with a spring in the handle
- small hacksaw
- ruler or yardstick
- large cardboard tube, wide enough to fit around the noodle
- thick paper, folded
- low-temperature mini-glue gun
- hole punch
- needle-nose pliers
- nail (smaller in diameter than the motor shaft)
- rock or hammer or drill with ¹⁄₃₂ bit (if no nail and hammer)
- wire stripper
- paintbrush
- heavy-duty diagonal pliers

Supplies Diagrams

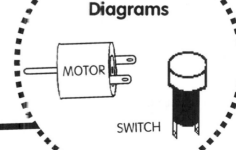

CAR FRAME AND WHEELS

INSTRUCTIONS

Step 1

With the scissors, **cut** a 4-by-6-inch or smaller piece from the corrugated cardboard or foam core (see diagram 1). Corrugated cardboard weighs less than foam core but bends where you may not want it to bend. Foam core is strong and tough but a little heavy. You want to keep the weight of the car as light as possible.

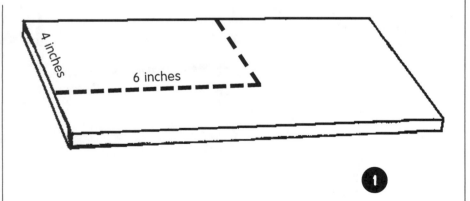

Step 2

In the center of one short end of the rectangle, **draw** then **cut** a notch 1½ to 2 inches wide and 3 to 3½ inches long (see diagram 2). The front tire will go into this slot.

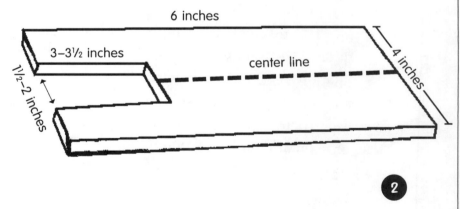

Step 3

With the diagonal cutters or needlenose pliers, **cut** a 10-inch length from the ¼-inch dowel. About ½ inch from the end of the car frame opposite the slot, **lay** the dowel, centered, across the car (see diagram 3a). The dowel is your axle. Securely **tape** it down using long strips of masking tape (see diagram 3b). **Smooth** the tape so it stays in place.

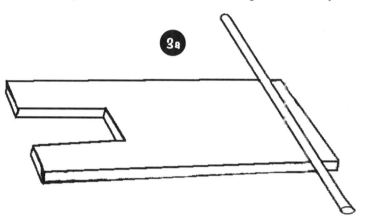

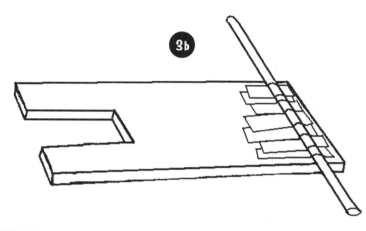

Step 4

Tape across the tape (see diagram 4). Make sure that the axle is secure. Don't glue the stick to the frame because you may need to adjust it later.

Step 5

Flip the frame over. The top of the car is now facing up (see diagram 5).

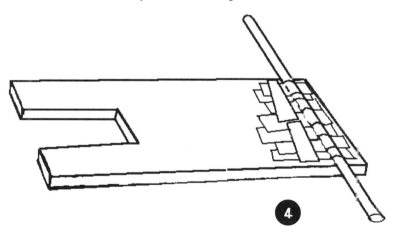

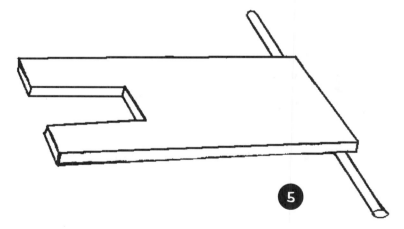

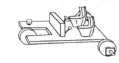

Step 6

Measure and **mark off** the noodle in several 1- to 2-inch increments for back tires and no more than 1-inch increments for front tires (see diagram 6). The front tire has to fit in the slot that you just cut into the front of the frame, with lots of room to turn.

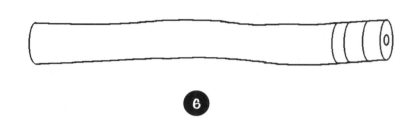

6

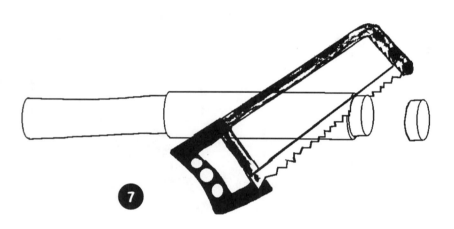

7

Slide the noodle through the cardboard tube until the first line you've drawn on the noodle aligns with the edge of the tube (see diagram 7). **Wedge** a folded piece of thick paper between the noodle and the tube to hold the tube steady. Keep one steadying hand firmly on the tube; with an adult holding the back of the hacksaw, use it **to cut** three wheels for each car from the noodle, the two back wheels 1 to 2 inches wide, the front wheel no wider than 1 inch. **Set** the front wheel aside for now.

Step 7

Step 8

Carefully **measure** to find the center of each back wheel (see diagram 8). If the hole is not in the center, then the car may not work as well. It's like having the brakes on all of the time. **Mark** the centers with a marker. Use a ¼-inch dowel to **punch** a hole in the middle of each back wheel (see diagram 8).

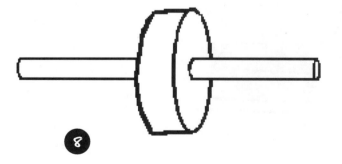

8

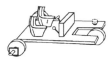

Important ....

Some noodles already have holes in the center, but they are larger than the diameter of the dowel—they work easily for the front wheel but you have to put hubcaps on them for the back wheels because the holes are too big for the dowel.

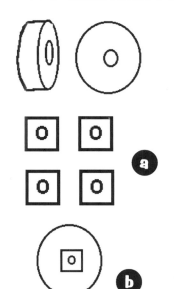

- **Cut** four 1-inch squares of cardboard. With the hole punch, **punch** a hole into the exact center of each (see diagram a).
- Use a glue gun to carefully **run** low-temperature glue around the hole in the wheel and **place** the cardboard over it. **Press** lightly until the hubcap stays on (see diagram b).
- **Flip** the wheel over and **repeat** with the other hubcap. Be sure to **align** the hole in the second hubcap with the hole in the first before you glue it down. If the wheel does not move freely when you put it on the axle, **twist** a chopstick, pencil, or the tip of the needle-nose pliers around in the holes to loosen them.

Step 9

From the cardboard or foam core, **cut** four 1-inch squares. With the hole punch, **punch** a hole in the center of each (see diagram 9a). **Place** one square on the axle on each side of the frame (see diagram 9b). Do not glue them. These two work as separators so that the wheels do not catch on the frame. **Slide** the wheels onto the dowel, then **slide** on the other two squares. **Tape** or **glue** around the hole to keep these two squares secure. The wheels should spin easily and have lots of room to move back and forth between the two separators (see diagram 9c). If they do not, **use** a dowel, chopstick, or pencil to enlarge the holes in the center of the wheels.

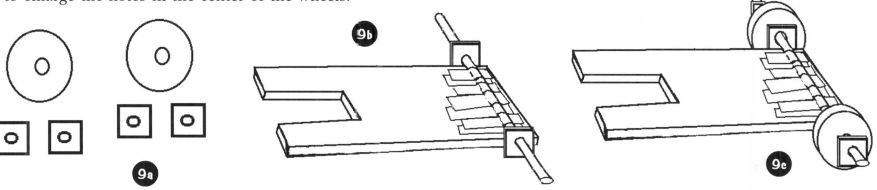

BATTERY PACK

INSTRUCTIONS

 **Cut** the flexible toilet paper tube lengthwise (see diagram 1).

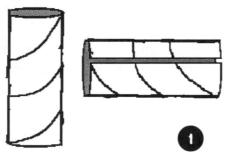

1

 **Cut** another lengthwise segment off 1 1/2 to 2 inches from one end (see diagram 2). Discard the piece.

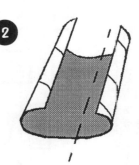

2

 **Work** with the remaining piece of toilet paper tube—roll it up, put some creases in it—to soften it up (see diagram 3).

 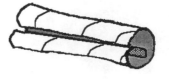

3

 **Roll** the piece into a tube around a marker about the same diameter as the AA batteries, (see diagram 4).

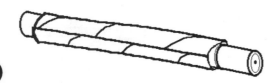

4

 **Unroll** the tube slightly, **run** some low-temperature glue along its edge, then **reroll** the tube (see diagram 5). **Remove** the marker. **Insert** one battery to make sure it fits loosely, but not too loosely.

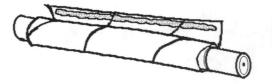

5

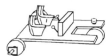

Step 6

Cut several strips of masking tape and **attach** the ends to your worktable to have them ready. **Wrap** the strips around the tube, covering its length to hold it securely (see diagram 6).

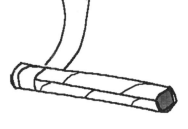

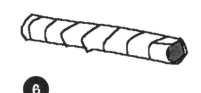

Step 7

On the piece of cereal box cardboard, use the marker to **trace** a circle using one end of the battery pack tube (see diagram 7a). **Cut** around the outside of the circle so it is slightly bigger than the end of the battery tube. With the pencil, **punch** a small hole directly in its center (see diagram 7b).

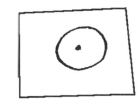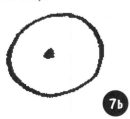

Step 8

Grab the end of the 22-gauge wire with a pair of needle-nose pliers. **Wrap** the wire up the pliers' tip to make a spring (see diagram 8a).

Cut the wire about 1½ inches below the spring (see diagram 8b). The wire is thin enough to cut with any scissors. Carefully **remove** the spring from the pliers.

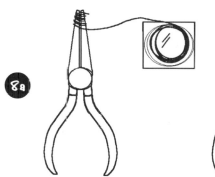

Step 9

Straighten the stem of the spring (see diagram 9a). **Push** the straight part of the wire through the hole in the cardboard circle so the spring rests on the plain side of the cardboard (the side that does not have a picture) (see diagram 9b). (Pictures peel off and can cause the battery pack to come apart.)

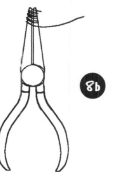

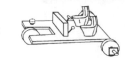

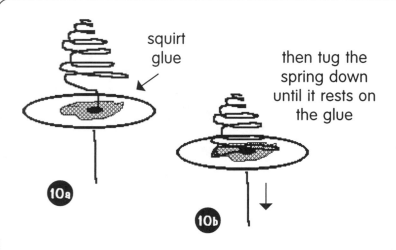

squirt glue

then tug the spring down until it rests on the glue

10a

10b

With the low-temperature glue gun, **squirt** glue on the cardboard under the spring (see diagram 10a). Plastic coating will keep the battery pack from working, so be careful not to get glue on top of the spiral of the spring or too far down on the stem. Gently **tug** the straight part of the wire until the bottom of the coil rests in the glue. Glue will also get on a small length of the straight edge, so the spring will be glued inside the hole as well. **Peel** off any stray glue after it has cooled.

Step 11

Trim the end of the toilet paper tube to make it nice and even. **Glue** the cardboard circle, spring inside, to the rim of the toilet paper tube (see diagram 11).

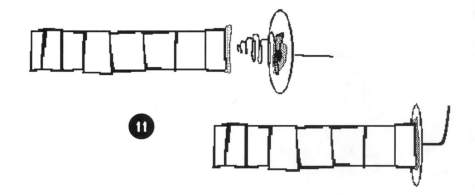

11

12

(⊖ BATTERY ⊕) (⊖ BATTERY ⊕)

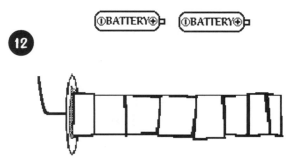

Step 12

After the glue is dry, **insert** the batteries with the negative end of one battery touching the positive end of the other (see diagram 12).

(⊕ BATTERY ⊖) (⊕ BATTERY ⊖)

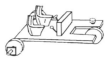

Step 13

Trim the tube almost to the edge of the batteries (see diagram 13). Don't cut too much off, but do cut enough so the copper wire in the cap you are going to make will touch the batteries.

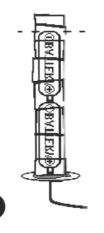

13

Step 14

Use a nail and hammer to **punch** a hole in the center top of the plastic cap (see diagram 14).

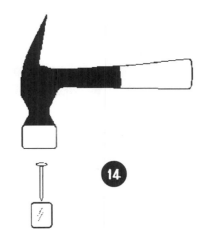

14

Step 15

Make another copper spring as you did in steps 7 and 8 (see diagram 15a). **Insert** the straight piece through the hole in the cap from the inside out (see diagram 15b). Glue the bottom of the spring into the cap.

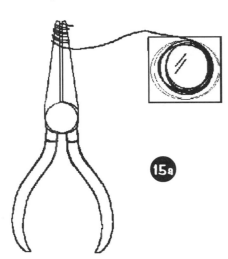

15a

15b

Note

If you don't have a plastic cap, use the strip of toilet paper tube. Cut a 1-inch strip and glue it into a ring. Cut a circle out of cereal box cardboard slightly larger than the end of the tube. Punch a hole in the center of the circle. Glue the circle to the tube, then glue the spring into it as above (see diagram). The ring has to be larger than the battery pack tube.

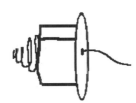

THREE-WHEELED MOTOR CAR

43

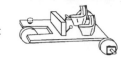

Place the cap on the open end of the battery pack tube (see diagram 16a). If it doesn't fit snugly, **remove** it and **wrap** masking tape around the end of the tube (see diagram 16b), replacing the cap frequently to make sure it fits snugly, but comes off easily (diagram 16c).

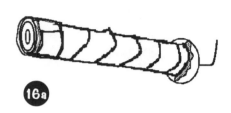

16a

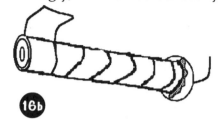

16b

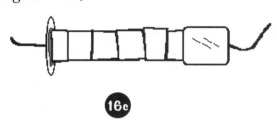

16c

Check that your battery pack works: **Attach** a piece of wire to each motor connector. **Touch** the end of each wire of your battery pack to each end of the wires attached to the motor.

If the motor doesn't hum and the spindle doesn't spin, check to make sure that you have inserted the batteries with negative touching positive, and that the copper springs are touching the batteries.

Tape the battery pack securely in front of and parallel to the axle with masking tape (see diagram 18). Do not put tape on the cap. **Tape** down your tape.

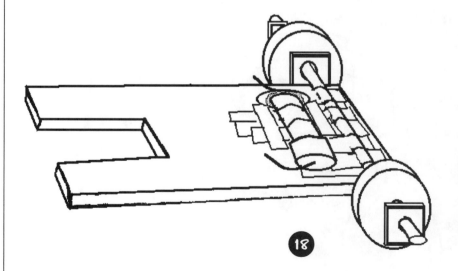

18

44

WIRING

INSTRUCTIONS

Step 1

Punch a hole on one side of the front of the car the size of the switch (see diagram 1). **Remove** the nut from the switch. **Insert** the switch into the hole, then **screw** the nut back on. I usually leave off the washer—the little ring on the switch between the nut and the bolt— because the cardboard is too thick.

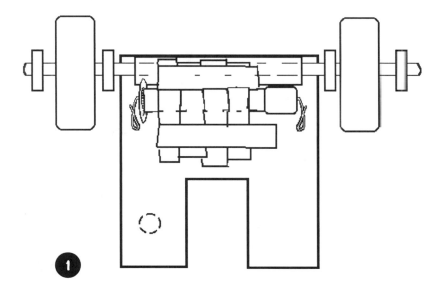

Step 2

Saw a ¹/₂- to ³/₄-inch piece from the ⁷/₈- to 1-inch dowel (see diagram 2a). Actually, any small piece of scrap wood works just as well. Dowels are made of hard wood and can crack easily. Use a hammer and nail or ask an adult to use a drill with a ¹/₃₂ bit or a headless nail attached to **drill** a hole through the center of the dowel piece (see diagram 2b).

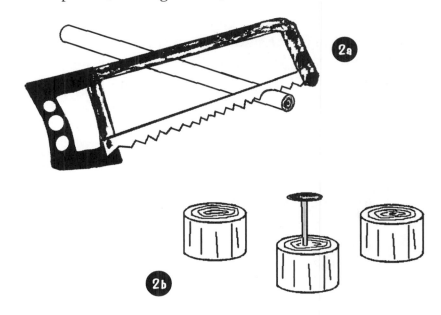

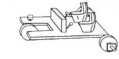

Push the rod on the motor into the hole in the dowel as you would push a thumbtack into a wall, leaving a small gap between the wood and the motor (see diagram 3). Don't push too fast or pull it out and push it back in. If the hole is too loose, the dowel will fly off the motor when it is turned on. If the dowel does fly off, replace it with a new piece of wood.

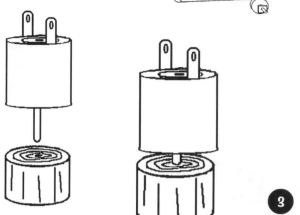

3

Step 4

Using a marker and the dowel piece, **trace** a circle onto the immediate center of the front tire (the pool noodle you cut and set aside earlier). **Cut** the circle out of the wheel, being careful not to cut it too big (see diagram 4a). **Run** some low-temperature glue around the inside of the hole, and **insert** the dowel piece inside (see diagram 4b). Do not get any glue on the motor or the wheel will not spin. If the noodle already has a large center hole, then just **glue** the dowel piece inside.

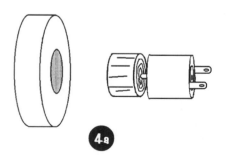

4a

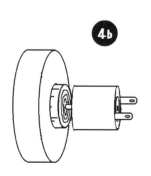

4b

Cut strips of masking tape long enough to go over the motor and attach to the bottom of the car on each side. **Place** the strips on the edge of your worktable, ready to use. **Put** one piece of tape on the motor. **Set** the motor on the opposite side from the switch at the front of the car, with the wheel inserted into the notch (see diagram 5). Make sure the wheel isn't touching anything. Friction will cause the motor to slow down or stop completely. **Smooth** your tape down right up against the motor so the motor does not wiggle.

Step 5

5

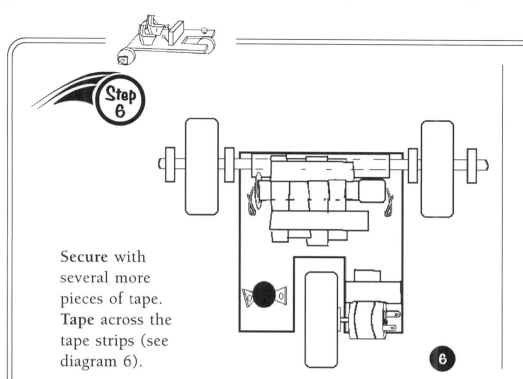

Step 6

Secure with several more pieces of tape. **Tape** across the tape strips (see diagram 6).

Step 7

Measure the distances between the battery pack and the switch, the switch and the motor, and the motor and the battery pack. **Add** at least two inches to each measurement. **Cut** one piece of 22-gauge coated electrical wire for each measurement (see diagram 7). With the wire stripper, **strip** the ends of each wire $^3/_4$ to 1 inch at each end.

Step 8

Tightly **twist** together one stripped end of the battery pack-to-switch wire with the wire extending from the cardboard circle of the battery pack. **Insert** the other stripped end into the hole on one prong of the switch; **twist** tightly (see diagram 8).

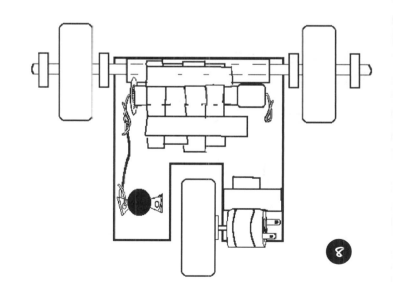

It is best to stick the wire through the hole in the post on the switch and motor, wrap the wire around the post, then twist it together (see diagram a). However, younger children may find it easier to slip it through the hole in the post, then twist it tightly together (see diagram b).

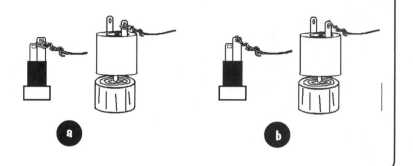

Step 9

Tightly **twist** together one stripped end of the battery pack-to-motor wire with the wire extending from the plastic cap on the battery pack. **Insert** the other stripped end through the hole on one prong of the motor (see diagram 9).

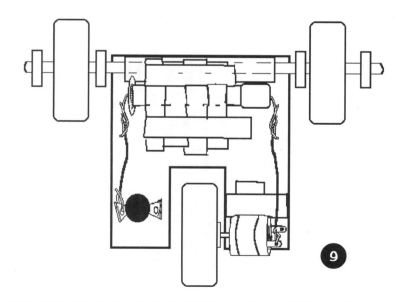

Step 10

Insert one stripped end of the remaining wire through the hole on the other prong on the switch. **Twist** tightly. Then **insert** the other end through the hole on the other prong of the motor (see diagram 10). **Twist** tightly.

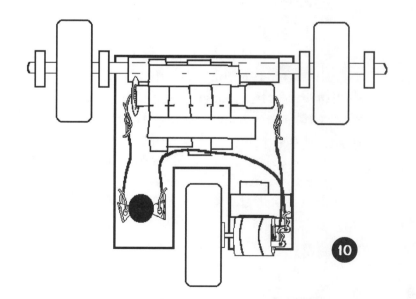

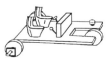

Step 11 Securely **tape** all covered wires down (see diagram 11). Be careful that the wires do not touch the wheel.

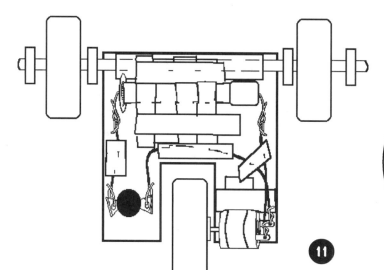

11

Step 12 **Turn** your car over and push the switch. If the car goes backward, take the batteries out and reverse them, being careful to keep positive to negative end. The spindle on the motor will turn in either direction.

WARNING
Do not put the wheels up against anyone's face or hair.

Step 13 **Paint** and **decorate** your car. **Add** lightweight egg-carton seats (see diagram 13).

TROUBLESHOOTING

- If the car is not running, you may need to push the battery pack cap more snugly onto the tube; it may have come loose.

- Squeeze the connections to make sure everything is touching.

- How can you make sure your batteries are good? Disconnect your motor from the switch and the battery pack. Lay one battery on the table. Touch each end with the wires connected to the motor. If the motor spins, the battery is good. Check the other battery in the same way.

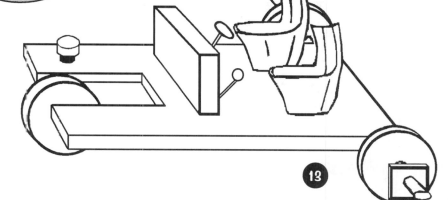

13

SCIENCE EXPERIMENT

Make two cars, one with a foam core base and the other with a corrugated cardboard base. Race them to record which is faster most often. Speculate on the reasons for the results.

CATAPULT

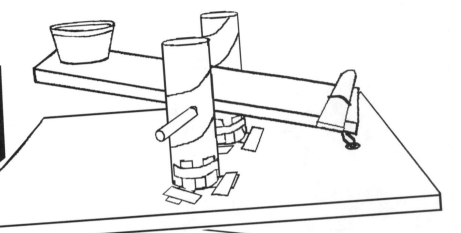

SUPPLIES

- one piece corrugated cardboard or foam core for the base
- two toilet paper tubes
- masking tape
- low-temperature mini-glue sticks
- ¼-inch dowel 8 to 10 inches long
- one stick of wood approximately 2 inches wide by 12 inches long or a plastic ruler
- one 12-inch pipe cleaner or heavy string
- one Popsicle or craft stick
- one size 18 or larger rubber band
- one small plastic, short, wide container, such as a sour cream or margarine tub, or a paper cup cut in half crosswise
- paint

TOOLS

- high-quality adult craft scissors with a spring in the handle
- low-temperature mini-glue gun
- hole punch
- heavy-duty diagonal cutting pliers
- marker or pencil
- nail
- hammer or rock
- paintbrush

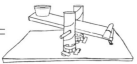

INSTRUCTIONS

Cut a piece of corrugated cardboard or foam core about 8 to 10 inches by 12 to 14 inches (see diagram 1).

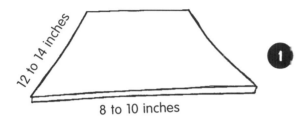

12 to 14 inches

8 to 10 inches

1

Place a hole punch as far down the side of the tube as it will go; **punch** two ¼-inch holes into the top of each tube, opposite each other. **Cut** a piece from the ¼-inch dowel long enough to go through both tubes with an inch or more extending on each side. **Insert** the dowel piece (see diagram 3). The dowel will be a fulcrum that supports the lever, allowing it to pivot so it can catapult objects through the air.

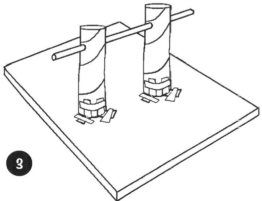

3

Place the toilet paper tubes upright in the center of the cardboard rectangle. They need to be about 2 inches plus about 2 finger widths apart. Glue tubes with the low-temperature glue gun to make the catapult last longer (see diagram 2). **Tape** the tubes to the base, then **tape** down your tape.

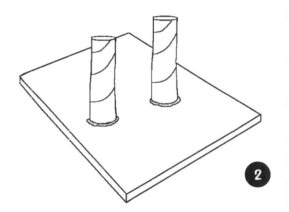

2

Step 4

Test the stick to make sure it is long enough by leaning it against the dowel. It should be long enough for one end to rest on the base with the other extending a few inches above the dowel (see diagram 6a).

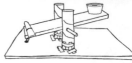

Step 5

Place a thick piece of scrap cardboard or wood under the stick so you don't damage the table; you are going to hammer the nail all the way through the wood. Use a hammer and nail to **punch** a hole about 1 inch from one end of the stick, large enough for the rubber band to go through (see diagram 5).

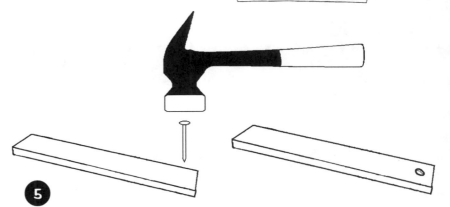

5

Step 6

Lean the stick against the dowel with the side with the hole resting on the base (see diagram 6a). Use a long pipe cleaner or strong string to **attach** the stick firmly to the dowel (see diagram 6b). The catapult will be more stable if you wrap the wire in an X pattern.

Note

You can use a plastic ruler if it has an existing hole in it. Note carefully the changes in the following steps if you do so.

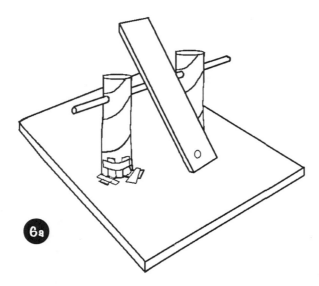

6a

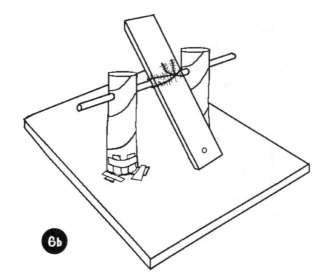

6b

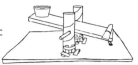

Step 7

Use scissors carefully to **punch** a hole through the base. The hole should match up somewhat with the hole in the board. The holes do not have to match up perfectly (see diagram 7).

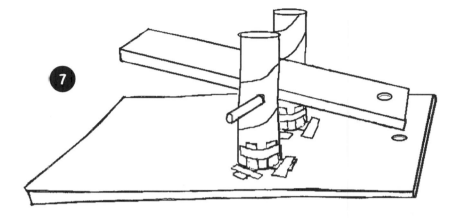

7

8a

8b

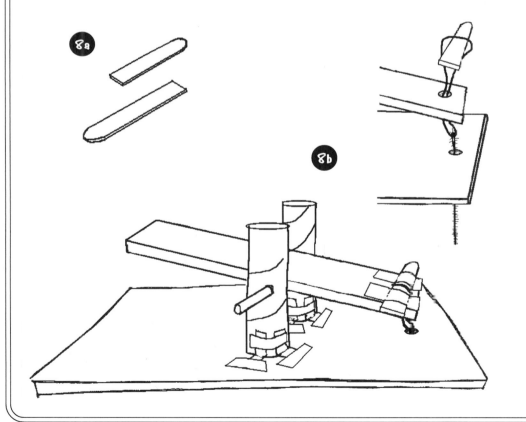

Step 8

Cut a Popsicle or craft stick in half crosswise (see diagram 8a). **Insert** one end of the rubber band through the hole in the board, then **insert** one-half of the craft stick through its loop (see diagram 8b). **Tape** it down with masking tape. **Push** the rubber band through the hole in the base. **Insert** the other half of the craft stick through that loop. **Tape** the stick to the underside of the base.

CATAPULT

Using a low-temperature glue gun, **glue** the plastic container or paper cup half about ¼ inch from the edge of the other end of the board (see diagram 9). Use a container that is relatively shallow so the things you catapult will not get stuck inside of it. The space behind the cup allows you to trigger the catapult with your finger.

Note
Use masking tape instead of the glue gun if you are using a plastic ruler.

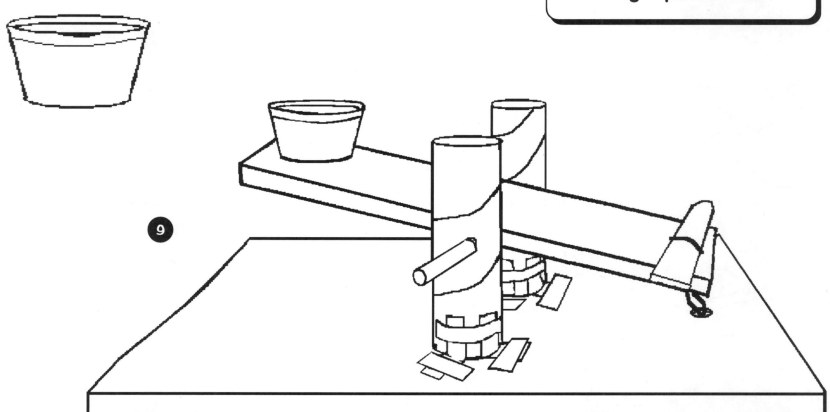

THINGS TO CATAPULT

SUPPLIES

- ✦ at least two egg carton cups
- ✦ paint, markers, and decorations

TOOLS

- ★ high-quality adult craft scissors with a spring in the handle
- ★ paintbrush

INSTRUCTIONS

Step 1

Trim the egg carton cups. **Glue** them together at the wide ends (see diagram 1).

❶

Step 2

Use paper and paint to **decorate** the cups as lightweight boulders, cats, rabbits, cows—whatever catches your fancy (see diagram 2).

❷

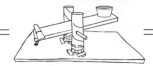

CATAPULT

ROCK CATAPULTS

Build the catapult base and fulcrum as in the main instructions. Instead of putting a hole and a rubber band through the stick, **wrap** a lot of masking tape around a rock. **Tape** the rock to the end of the stick that would have had the hole in it. **Attach** the stick to the fulcrum as in the earlier instructions. **Lift** the rock off of the base, **place** something in the plastic container, then **release** the rock (it should thud against the base). Catapult light-weight objects across the room. Marshmallows would be fun.

Note
A plastic ruler will not work as the stick in this catapult.

TROUBLESHOOTING

If the egg carton characters do not fly out of the cup, then the cup is either too tall or too skinny. Try larger containers.

QUICK AND EASY CATAPULTS

Use a flexible plastic spoon and a plastic bottle, such as a vitamin bottle. **Remove** the lid. **Glue** the bottle on its side to a corrugated cardboard base. **Tape** the pill bottle to the base. **Glue**, then **tape** the spoon upright against the pill bottle, handle against the base. **Lay** the lid against the spoon handle on the base. **Glue**, then **tape** the lid against the handle to keep the spoon in place. **Place** an egg-carton character in the spoon top, then **pull** back gently and release.

SCIENCE AND MATH EXPERIMENTS

Slide the wooden stick or ruler up or down the fulcrum to change the angle between the stick and the ground. See if larger angles increase or decrease the firing range of your catapult. The change in angle will also change the height at which the object flies. If you were trying to get an object over a castle wall, what would be more important: the height or the distance an object will fly?

BOBBING DOG

SUPPLIES

- paper egg carton cup
- cereal box cardboard or other lightweight cardboard
- one Popsicle or craft stick
- items to create dog's features (ears, eyes, nose, tail)
- one small rock or large bead
- marker or pencil
- low-temperature mini-glue sticks
- thread
- one pipe cleaner
- paint
- items to create features such as tails and feet

TOOLS

- high-quality adult craft scissors with a spring in the handle
- heavy-duty cutting pliers
- low-temperature mini-glue gun
- hole punch
- pencils
- paintbrush

INSTRUCTIONS

Step 1

With the scissors, **cut** an arch in each side of an egg carton cup until it looks like it has four legs (see diagram 1a). **Cut** one arch a little higher at the front for the neck hole (see diagram 1b).

Step 2

Cut a circle of cardboard that will fit snugly into the egg carton cup right below the lowest arch. Measure as you trim (see diagram 2).

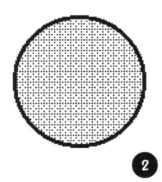

Step 3

With the pliers, cut the Popsicle or craft stick in half crosswise (see diagram 3).

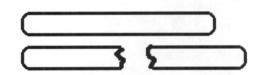

Step 4

Decorate the round end of the stick to look like a dog (see diagram 4).

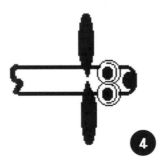

Step 5

Glue the small rock to the cut end of the Popsicle stick (see diagram 5). The rock is your counterweight.

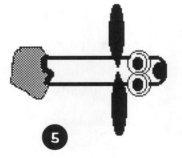

 **Step 6**

Find the center of gravity of the stick: **Place** your finger under the stick at a point between the rock and the head. If the stick does not balance, **move** your finger and **try** again until the stick balances on your finger. With a marker or a pencil, **mark** the spot where your finger balanced the stick. With a low-temperature glue gun, **put** a little glue on the mark and **wrap** the string around the stick (see diagram 6).

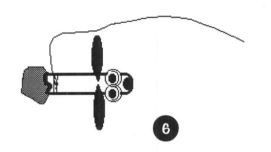

 **Step 7**

After the glue dries, **hold** the end of the string to make sure the head and rock are still balanced (see diagram 7). If not, **add** more glue to either end.

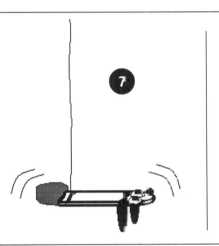

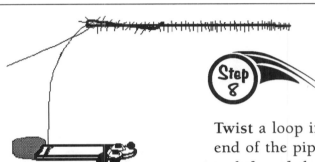

 **Step 8**

Twist a loop in the end of the pipe cleaner and **thread** the string through the loop (see diagram 8).

 **Step 9**

With a pencil, **punch** a little hole at the top of the egg carton cup (see diagram 9a). **Poke** the pipe cleaner up through the hole in the egg carton cup (see diagram 9b). **Pull** the string through until the dog's head is under the neck hole; be sure you get the head in the highest arch.

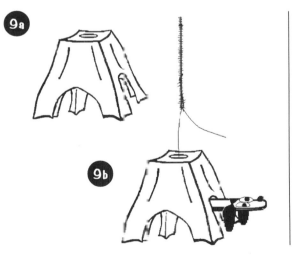

Step 10

Glue the string to the outside top of the carton cup; **cut** off the extra (see diagram 10).

Glue the edges of the circle of cardboard inside the cup about the height of the leg arches, but below the craft stick. Make sure that the stick or rock does not rest on the circle of cardboard (see diagram 11).

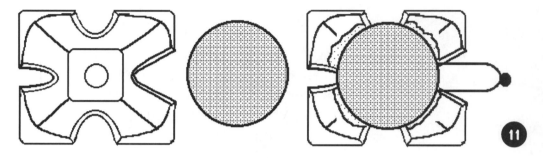

11

Paint the egg carton cup to look like a dog. **Add** feet and a tail (see diagram 12). **Set** it in your hand and watch the head bob up and down.

12

OTHER ANIMALS

What can you make besides a dog? How about building a cat, turtle, rabbit, or even a fish or a snake looking out of a hole?

MATH OR SCIENCE APPLICATION

This project is great for teaching about weights and balances.

THE DUCK THAT LAYS A GOLDEN EGG

SUPPLIES

- ◆ one 1-gallon milk jug or other gallon container with a similar shape
- ◆ pencil or marker
- ◆ one 4- to 5-inch plastic lid
- ◆ low-temperature mini-glue sticks
- ◆ four size 16 or 18 rubber bands
- ◆ two Popsicle or craft sticks
- ◆ masking tape
- ◆ one 2- to 5-inch Styrofoam ball (or something else for a head)
- ◆ cereal box or construction paper for a beak or a snout
- ◆ corrugated cardboard for feet and top of legs
- ◆ two toilet paper tubes
- ◆ items for adding features such as feathers
- ◆ paint
- ◆ plastic eggs

TOOLS

- ★ high-quality adult craft scissors with a spring in the handle
- ★ hole punch
- ★ heavy-duty diagonal-cutting pliers
- ★ marker or pencil
- ★ heart-shaped pattern (page 66)
- ★ low-temperature mini-glue gun
- ★ paintbrush

INSTRUCTIONS

Step 1

Thoroughly **clean** the gallon container.

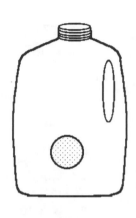

Step 2

On the side of the jug by the handle, **draw** a 2-inch diameter circle in the middle of the flat area (see diagram 2). Have an adult **poke** a hole in the middle of it so you can **cut** it out. This side is the top of the jug, where you insert the egg.

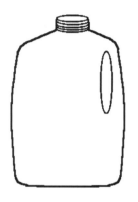

Step 3

On the opposite side of the jug, **trace** the plastic lid (see diagram 3). **Cut** the circle out.

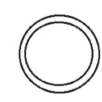

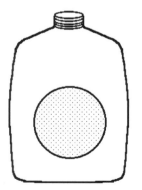

Step 4

With an adult's help and pushing the hole punch as far as it will go over the plastic, **punch** four holes in the plastic jug one above, below, and to each side of the large hole (see diagram 4).

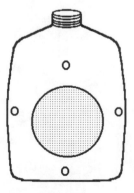

 **Step 5**

Draw a plus sign on the plastic lid, with the intersection in the exact center of the lid (see diagram 5a). Use the hole punch to **punch** a hole at the end of each line (see diagram 5b).

5a

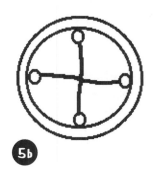
5b

 **Step 6**

Push one end of a rubber band through each hole in the lid. Then **insert** one loop through the other loop (see diagram 6).

6

 **Step 7**

Pull the rubber bands tight (see diagram 7). If they don't stay snug in the holes, don't worry; you can push them back into the holes when you are putting the duck together.

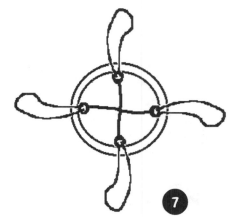
7

 **Step 8**

Use the heavy-duty pliers to **cut** the Popsicle or craft sticks in half crosswise (see diagram 8).

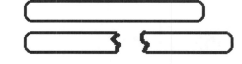

8

Step 9

Line up the holes in the plastic lid with the holes by the large hole in the jug (see diagram 9). **Squeeze** the lid slightly and place it in the large hole (see diagram 9). **Pull** the free end of each rubber band from the inside out through each hole in the jug (see diagram 9).

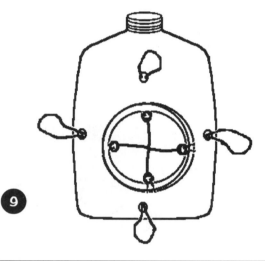

Step 10

Put one stick through the loop in a rubber band. **Pull** the stick up until the rubber band is tight, then **tape** the stick down with masking tape (see diagram 10). **Repeat** with the three other rubber bands and stick halves, taping the bottom stick to the bottom of the jug and the side sticks to the sides.

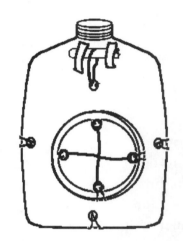

Step 11

Glue the polystyrene ball to the mouth of the jug (see diagram 11).

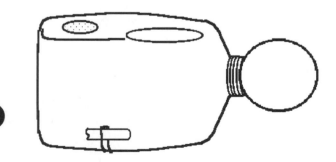

Step 12

Draw a beak on the cardboard or construction paper. **Cut** it out, then **fold** it (see diagram 12).

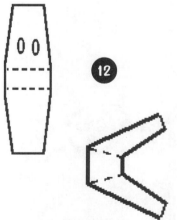

Step 13

Using low-temperature glue and masking tape where appropriate, **add** features (eyes, ears, the beak, and so on) to the head (see diagram 13). Don't add too much; the head cannot be too heavy or the animal will tip forward.

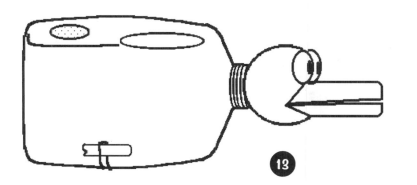

13

14

Trace the pattern (page 66) onto the corrugated cardboard. You can make the feet larger, if you'd like. **Draw** some U shapes to make toes (see diagram 14). **Cut** along the lines. **Notch** the bottom of the heart to look like two heels (see diagram 14).

Step 14

Step 15

Cut the two toilet paper tubes lengthwise (see diagram 15a). **Roll** them up thin enough to look like duck legs (see diagrams 15b and 15c). Do not cut the tubes shorter because you need enough clearance for the eggs to drop later. **Wrap** masking tape around each one to hold it together and strengthen it (see diagram 15d).

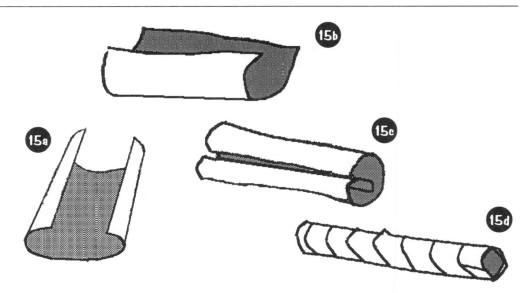

15b

15a

15c

15d

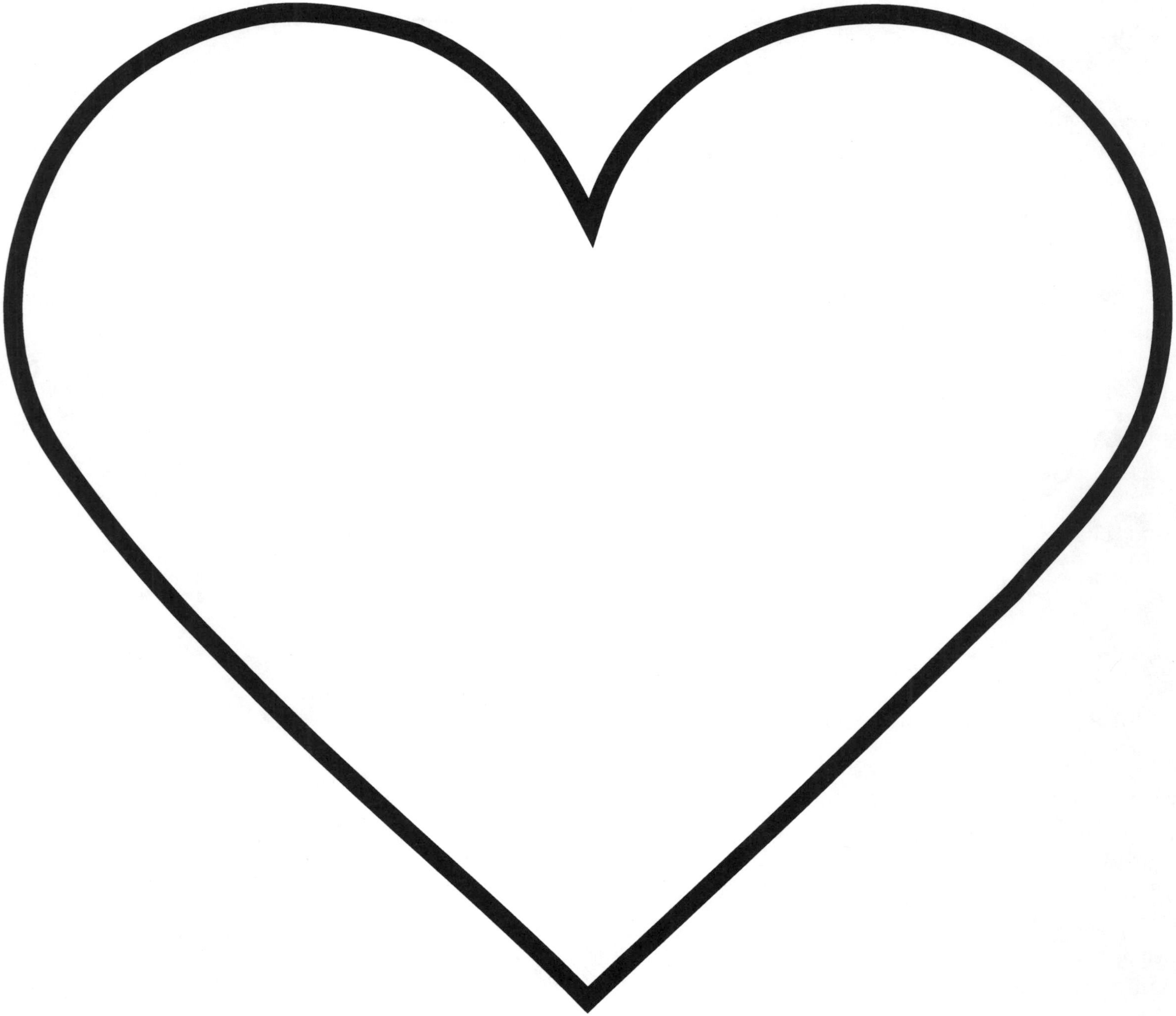

 **Step 16**

Glue both legs upright and close together to the top of the feet (see diagrams 16a and 16b).

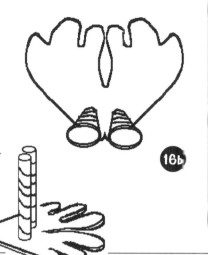

16b

16a

 **Step 17**

17a

Cut an oval just smaller than your plastic lid out of the corrugated cardboard (see diagram 17a). **Glue** the oval to the top of the legs (see diagram 17b). The oval makes it easier to attach the legs to the plastic lid.

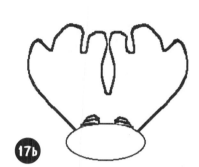

17b

 **Step 18**

Put one hand through the hole in the plastic jug that you made for the egg (see diagram 18a). The plastic lid attached with rubber bands is on the side opposite your hand. **Spread** your fingers around the rim of the plastic lid to support the lid from the inside of the carton. With your other hand and the low-temperature glue gun, **apply** glue to the center of the outside of the lid. **Press** the oval piece of cardboard that is connected to the legs into the glue and **hold** it steady until it dries. **Tape** around the oval cardboard to hold it more securely. **Tape** crosswise over the pieces of tape (see diagram 18b).

18b

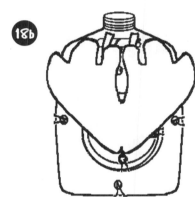

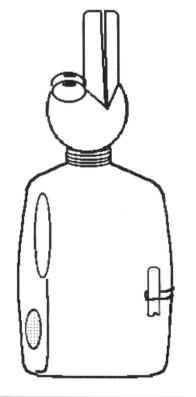

18a

Warning
Avoid applying glue to the areas where your fingers are inside the jug so you don't burn yourself.

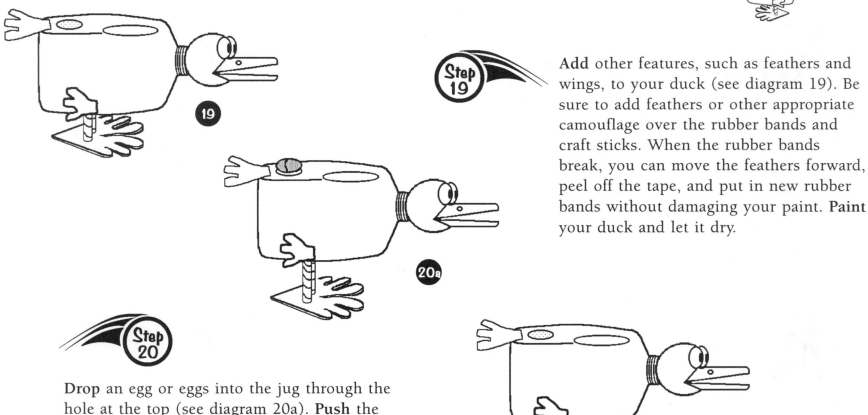

Step 19

Add other features, such as feathers and wings, to your duck (see diagram 19). Be sure to add feathers or other appropriate camouflage over the rubber bands and craft sticks. When the rubber bands break, you can move the feathers forward, peel off the tape, and put in new rubber bands without damaging your paint. **Paint** your duck and let it dry.

Step 20

Drop an egg or eggs into the jug through the hole at the top (see diagram 20a). **Push** the body to the ground, then let it go. When it comes back up, an egg will be on the ground by its feet (see diagram 20b)!

TROUBLESHOOTING

. . . .

If the egg does not come out easily, you may have too much tension in your rubber bands (they may be stretched too tightly to release easily). Move and reattach the sticks closer to the holes, or you may need to cut the bottom hole of the duck a little bigger.

OTHER ANIMALS

. . . .

With a little imagination and a lot of fun, you can make an alligator, dinosaur, chicken, spider, or any other life form that lays eggs. How about a space creature? You'll have to use something that resembles the head of your creature and other appropriate features.

FERRIS WHEEL

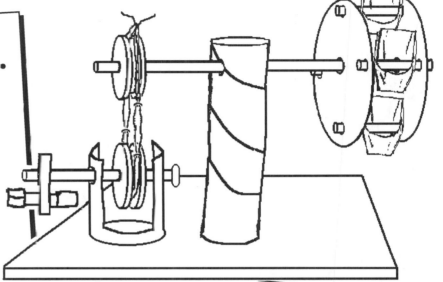

SUPPLIES

- one large piece of corrugated cardboard or foam core
- low-temperature mini-glue sticks
- paper towel tube
- masking tape
- one ¼-inch dowel 36 inches long (or pieces left over from other projects)
- one swimming pool noodle
- one half-gallon plastic milk jug, oatmeal container, or something of similar size
- pencil or marker
- five to eight size 18 rubber bands
- two heavy-duty paper plates, cereal box cardboard, or something similar
- one egg carton or other appropriate containers
- pipe cleaners, craft sticks, tongue depressors, or anything else in your scraps
- paint

TOOLS

- high-quality adult craft scissors with spring in handle
- low-temperature mini-glue gun
- hole punch
- hacksaw
- nail
- hammer or rock
- paintbrush
- heavy-duty diagonal cutting pliers

BASE AND POLE

INSTRUCTIONS

 **Step 1**

Cut a rectangle at least 12 by 15 inches from the cardboard or foam core (see diagram 1). The size is really up to you; the base just needs to be big enough to hold the wheel, pulley, and crank side by side.

1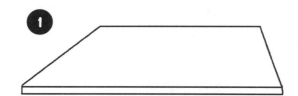

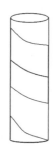 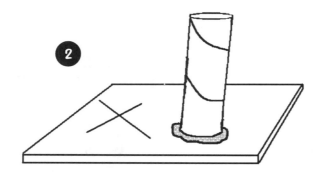
2

Use the low-temperature glue gun to **attach** the paper towel tube upright to the base. **Leave** enough space on the base for the crank to be placed beside the tube and about 2 inches from one edge if you are going to add the crank and pulley (see diagram 2). Add extra glue around the outside of the tube to make the attachment stronger (see diagram 2).

Step 2

 **Step 3**

Tape the edges of the tube down with medium-length strips of tape. Be sure your pieces are long enough to extend up the tube as well as out onto the base a bit (see diagram 3). Without tape it will snap off at the base. The tape should be flat against the base and paper towel tube. **Smooth** the tape down with your fingers so there are no gaps or air holes, especially at the base. **Run** your fingers around the base to create a closer seal.

3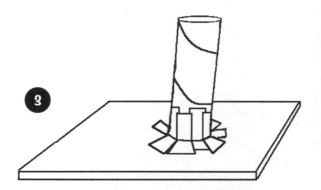

Step 4

Place strips of tape crosswise over the other strips of tape on the base and on the tube (see diagram 4). The Ferris wheel is heavy and will put a lot of stress on the tube. To keep it from breaking off later, it is a good idea to **make** the connection to the base as strong as possible.

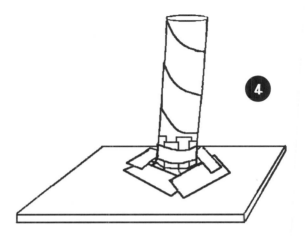

4

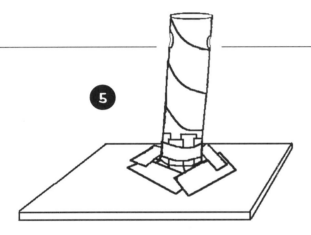

5

Step 5

Push the hole punch over the top of the tube as far as it will go on the side that faces the width of the base. **Punch** one hole. **Punch** another in the same manner directly opposite the first hole (see diagram 5). The farther down the holes, the less likely the wheel will tear off.

Step 6

With diagonal cutters, **cut** the dowel 12 inches long if you are not going to use the pulley (see following steps). **Cut** the dowel 16 inches long if you are going to use the pulley. **Insert** the dowel through the holes in the tube (see diagram 6). Remember to **leave** enough space under the dowel on the base for the pulley if you are going to build the pulley and crank.

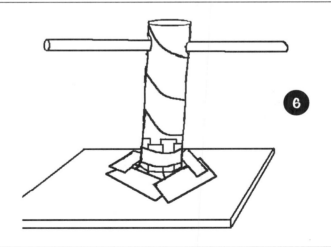

6

CRANK

INSTRUCTIONS

 **Step 1**

Cut a 1-by-1½-inch rectangle out of corrugated cardboard, foam core, or something with similar strength. **Punch** two holes in it (see diagram 1).

1

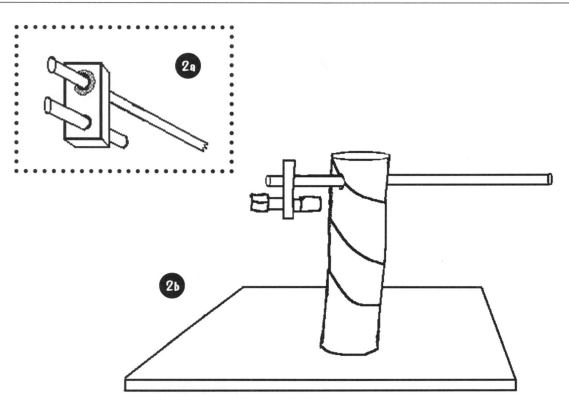

2a

2b

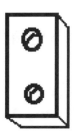 **Step 2**

Place one hole in the small piece of cardboard over the dowel that is in the tube (see diagram 2a). **Run** low-temperature glue around the dowel to glue it to the small piece of cardboard. **Cut** a 2-inch piece of dowel or use a scrap piece of dowel. **Push** it through the remaining hole in the cardboard. Do not glue it. **Wrap** tape around both ends to keep the stick from falling out of the hole (see diagram 2b). This mechanism is your hand crank.

PULLEY

INSTRUCTIONS

Step 1

With a hacksaw, **cut** two 1½- to 3-inch-wide circles from a swimming pool noodle (see diagram 1).

1

Step 2

With the tips of the scissors, **cut** a groove into both wheels all the way around (see diagram 2). The groove should be wide enough to hold a rubber band loosely so it can move back and forth, and deep enough to keep it from popping off the wheel.

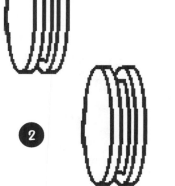

2

Step 3

Use a dowel or pencil to **poke** a hole through the center of the two wheels (see diagram 3).

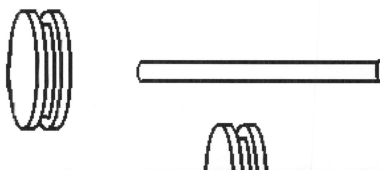

3

Step 4

Cut enough off the top of the milk jug or oatmeal box for the bottom part to fit under the dowel in the paper towel tube (see diagram 4a). If it is a milk jug, you will probably need to cut it in half. Double-check that the container fits under the dowel with room to spare (see diagram 4b).

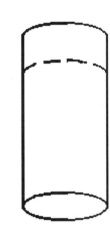

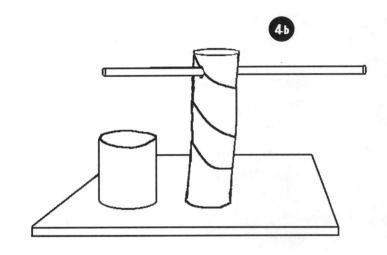

Step 5

Leaving at least 1 inch on the bottom, **cut** two deep rectangles across from each other out of the front and the back of the box (see diagram 5). **Leave** enough on the sides for a stick to go through.

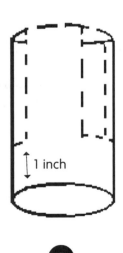

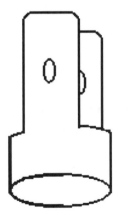

Step 6

Push the hole punch over the top of each side as far as possible. **Punch** one hole in the top of each side directly across from each other (see diagram 6).

Step 7

Cut a piece of dowel long enough to go through the holes in the carton with an overlap of 1 inch on one side and 3 inches on the other (the diameter of the container plus 4 inches; see diagram 7).

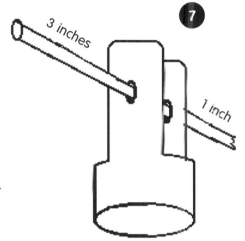
3 inches

1 inch

7

Step 8

Insert the dowel through one hole in the container, then through a wheel, then through the other side of the container (see diagram 8).

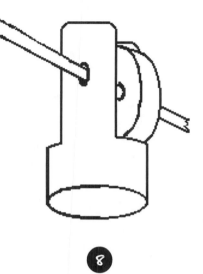
8

Step 9

Cut a 1-by-1½-inch rectangle out of corrugated cardboard, foam core, or something with similar strength. **Punch** two holes large enough for the dowel (see diagram 9).

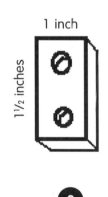
1 inch

1½ inches

9

Step 10

Place one hole over the 3-inch extension of the dowel that is in the tube (see diagram 10). **Glue** the dowel into the hole in the small piece of cardboard. **Cut** a 2-inch piece of dowel or use a scrap piece of dowel. **Push** it through the bottom hole in the cardboard. Do not glue it. **Wrap** tape around both ends to keep the dowel from falling out of the hole (see diagram 10).

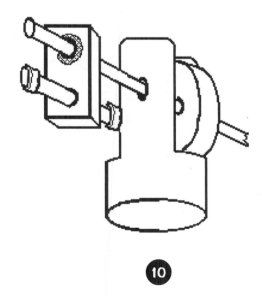
10

Wrap a piece of tape or place a small square of cardboard or foam core with a hole punched in the center on the other end of the long dowel to keep it from sliding out (see diagram 11). **Attach** it with low-temperature glue.

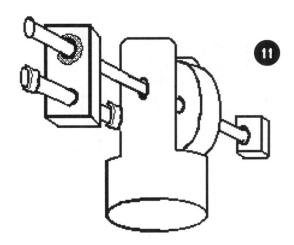

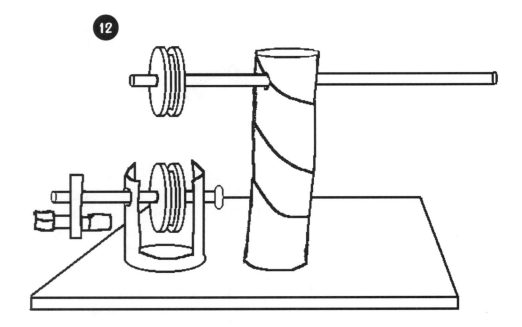

Place the other wheel on the long dowel that is extending through the tube. **Set** the container on the base of the Ferris wheel under the extended dowel. **Align** the grooves in the two wheels (see diagram 12). When you get the wheels aligned, **trace** the bottom of the container so you can replace it exactly where you have it. **Remove** the container, squeeze glue onto the bottom, and set it back on the outlined shape. **Tape** it to the base as you did the tube. **Glue** the wheels to the dowels after making sure they align.

BELT

INSTRUCTIONS

Step 1 — Put the end of one rubber band through another rubber band (see diagram 1a). Then **put** one loop through the other loop on the same rubber band (see diagram 1b). **Tighten** (see diagram 1c). **Continue** connecting rubber bands in this manner (about five or six), checking the length as you go to ensure the belt will fit around both wheels. The belt should be tight enough to stay on the wheels but loose enough to allow the wheels to move when you turn the crank.

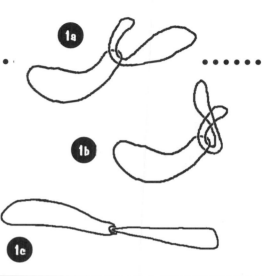

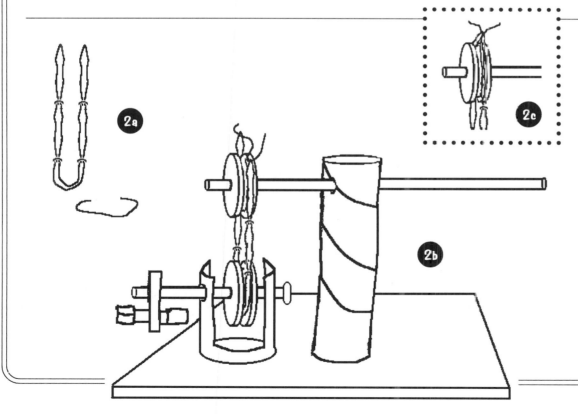

Step 2 — When your belt is long enough, **cut** the last rubber band (see diagram 2a). **Hold** the cut ends of the rubber band together in one hand. **Wrap** the belt around the bottom wheel and pull it up around the top wheel (see diagram 2b). **Insert** one cut end of the last rubber band through the circle of the rubber band it meets (see diagram 2c). **Tie** the cut ends of the rubber band together; **tighten** until the belt is tight enough to stay on the wheels but will allow the wheels to move. Your crank, pulley, and base should look like diagram 2b.

THE WHEEL

INSTRUCTIONS

Cut the centers (before the plate starts to curve up) out of two heavy-duty paper plates (see diagram 1). Or cut two circles the size of the center of a 9-inch paper plate out of cereal boxes or similar material.

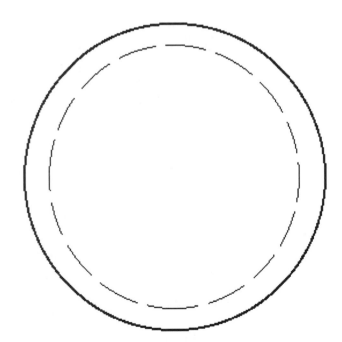

1

Step 2

Stack the circles on top of each other. **Punch** a ¼-inch hole (large enough for the dowel) through the exact center of both circles (see diagram 2). **Separate** the circles.

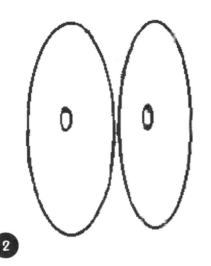

2

Step 3

On one circle, with a pencil, lightly **draw** a plus sign that intersects at the hole. **Mark** one dot on each line about 1 inch in from the edge of the circle (see diagram 3).

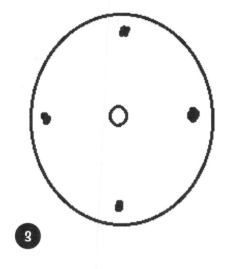

3

Step 4

Use a hole punch to **punch** holes where you marked the dots (see diagram 4).

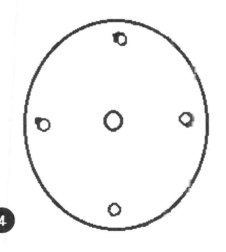

4

Step 5

Put the two circles back together (see diagram 5), lining up the center holes.

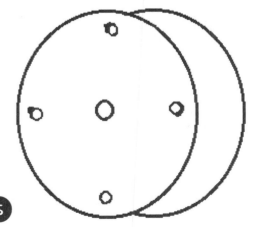

5

Step 6

With the center holes of the circles lined up, use a marker to **color** through the punched-out holes of one circle to **mark** dots in the same places on the other circle (see diagram 6). Use a hole punch to **punch** out the holes. The holes in one circle should line up perfectly with the holes in the other.

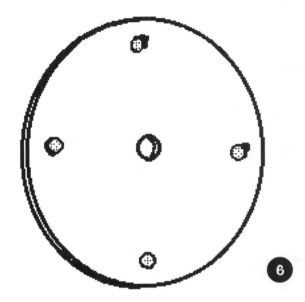

6

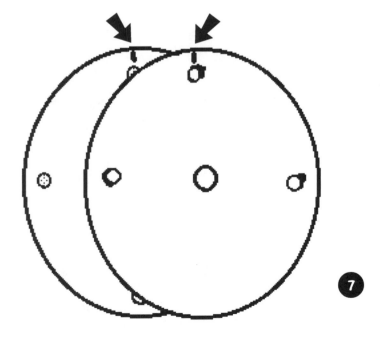

7

Step 7

Mark above one hole in the top circle, then **mark** above the corresponding hole in the second circle (see diagram 7). You'll know to always align these two holes first, then the rest should line up, as well.

Step 8

Use any small, lightweight containers for the seats. I like to use egg carton cups. **Trim** four egg-carton containers to look like seats (see diagram 8a). **Punch** a ¼-inch hole on each side of the chair; the holes should be directly across from each other (see diagram 8b). With a pencil, make the holes larger if you want the seats to swing.

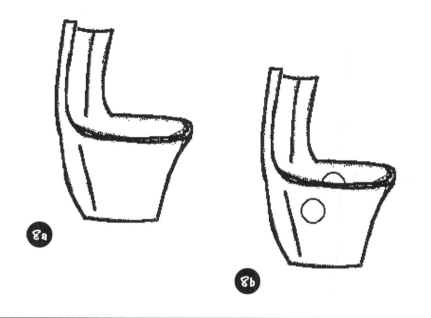

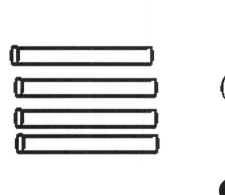

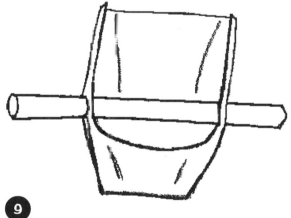

Step 9

Cut four 3-inch dowel pieces. **Push** one dowel piece through the holes in each egg carton seat. The ends of the dowel should extend slightly on either side (see diagram 9).

 **Step 10**

Slide the center holes of the two circles onto the dowel extending from the tube opposite the pulley (see diagram 10).

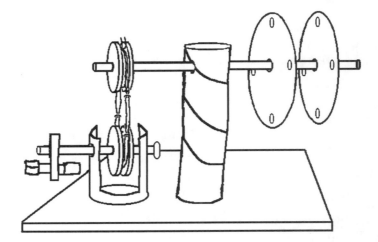

10

 **Step 11**

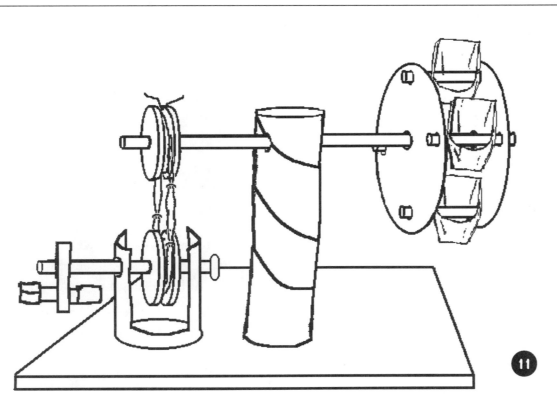

11

Slide each dowel with the egg carton seat between the wheels, then into a matched set of holes on the large circles. **Glue** the ends of the dowels to the circles with low-temperature glue. **Glue** each circle's center hole to the long dowel. The Ferris wheel should look like the one in diagram 11. **Turn** the crank to see it work.

Step 12

Paint your Ferris wheel. **Make** people out of the scraps you have collected. **Name** your Ferris wheel something fun: Twister, Thriller, the Fun Trap. **Make** a sign. **Make** a ticket booth and **paint** it.

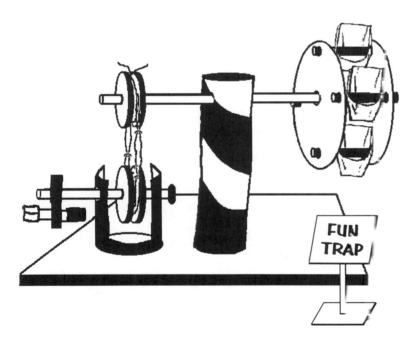

TROUBLESHOOTING

If the belt slides off the wheels or gets caught in the grooves of the pulley, first make sure the wheels are lined up. If they are and the problem still occurs, cut the grooves in the wheels wider and deeper. If the tube holes tear, glue a 3-inch section of toilet paper tube under the holes to reinforce them.

SCIENCE PROJECTS

Using the pulley and crank to spin the Ferris wheel is called *power conversion*. You take the power of one object (the pulley) and convert it into power for another object (the wheel). Answer the following questions:

- Which wheel spins faster at its outside edge, the small pulley wheel or the large Ferris wheel? Why?
- Try other materials for the belt, for example elastic or heavy string. What materials work best?
- Try other objects for the pulley wheels, for example, a spool. Do they work well? Why or why not?
- Make the pulley wheels different sizes. Does this difference change the speed of the Ferris wheel?
- What else can you power using a pulley?

MERRY-GO-ROUND

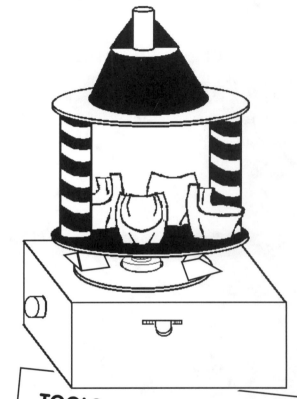

SUPPLIES

- two paper plates or cereal box cardboard
- three toilet paper tubes
- low-temperature mini-glue sticks
- masking tape
- four egg carton cups or other containers for seats
- paint
- beads, pipe cleaners, paper, yarn to make people
- two AA batteries
- marker or pencil
- cereal box or other lightweight cardboard
- 22- to 24-gauge copper electrical wire
- one plastic cap from a sport water bottle
- 1.5- to 3-volt DC motor
- one square or rectangular box at least 5 inches long for the base, strong enough to hold merry-go-round without sagging in the middle
- push-on push-off switch
- two or three Popsicle or craft sticks
- one 2-by-2-by-1/4-inch block of wood
- 22-gauge coated copper electrical wire
- scrap cardboard or polystyrene from egg carton for brakes
- one 4- to 5-inch plastic lid or cardboard circle

TOOLS

- high-quality adult craft scissors with a spring in the handle
- low-temperature mini-glue gun
- paintbrush
- needle-nose pliers
- wire stripper

CIRCLES AND POSTS

INSTRUCTIONS

Step 1

Cut a 6-inch circle from the center of two paper plates or **trace** and **cut** out two 6-inch circles on the front and back of a cereal box (see diagram 1).

Step 2

Cut the three toilet paper tubes lengthwise (see diagram 2a). Then make a lengthwise cut about 1½ inches from the edge of the open tubes (see diagram 2b).

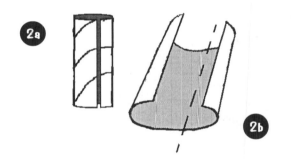

Step 3

Roll two tubes up as fat or thin as you would like your merry-go-round posts to be (see diagram 3a). **Apply** low-temperature glue to the edges to secure. **Cut** off long strips of masking tape and **attach** them to the edge of your worktable to have them ready. **Wrap** the strips around the tubes, covering their lengths to hold them securely (see diagrams 3b and 3c).

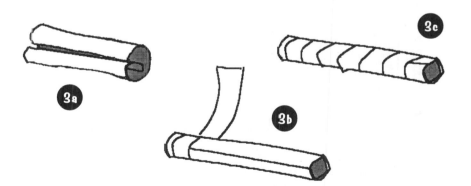

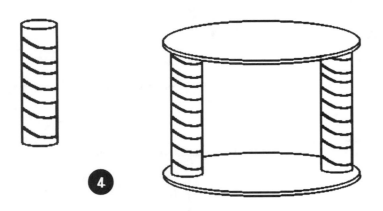

4

Step 4

Trim the posts until they are about 4 inches tall or shorter to keep the merry-go-round from being top heavy. **Glue** one post ¼ inch from the edge on top of one cardboard circle. **Glue** the other post opposite the first about ¼ inch in from the edge (see diagram 4). **Glue** the second circle on top of the posts (see diagram 4).

Step 5

Trim the four egg carton cups to look like chairs (see diagram 5). **Glue** them to the lower circle, facing outward.

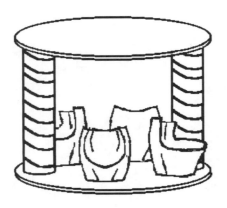

5

Step 6

Paint your merry-go-round and decorate it with markers. You might also want to **add** some light decorations to the top (see diagram 6). **Make** people to go in the cars.

6

BATTERY PACK

INSTRUCTIONS

See car battery pack, pages 40–44.

Check that your battery pack works: **Attach** a piece of wire to each motor connector. **Touch** the end of each wire of your battery pack to each end of the wires attached to the motor. If the motor doesn't hum and the spindle doesn't spin, **check** to make sure that you have inserted the batteries with negative touching positive, and that the copper springs are touching the batteries.

BASE

INSTRUCTIONS

If necessary, **cut** the bottom or top off your box so you can easily access the inside. **Find** an object that is about as big as the push button on your switch. **Trace** around the object in the center of one end of the box. **Cut** out the circle. **Find** another object that is roughly the same diameter as the motor. **Trace** around it in the center of the top of the box. **Cut** out that hole. You want the switch and motor to fit snugly into their holes. If you cut the holes too big, you can cut a circle patch from cardboard, cut the right-sized hole in the patch, then glue it over the original hole.

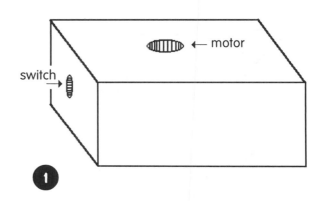

switch

← motor

1

Step 2 From the inside of the box, **insert** the switch into the side of the box with the button extending out of the hole (see diagram 2a). From the inside, **insert** the motor into the top hole, spindle side up (see diagram 2a). **Hold** the motor and **adjust** it until it is sticking out of the box only as far as you want it to, but not more than ¼ inch. Carefully **mark** a line on the motor at the box. **Take** out the motor and **measure** down from the line so you know how much of the motor will be hidden in the box. Measure exactly. On either side of the box, and directly across from the hole for the motor, **measure** that same amount down from the top of the box and **mark** a horizontal line. **Cut** a horizontal slit wide enough to snugly hold the craft stick on each side (see diagram 2b). If the motor is too wobbly, then **cut** a circle of corrugated cardboard and **cut** a hole in the center of it the size of the motor. **Glue** it to your box to add stability.

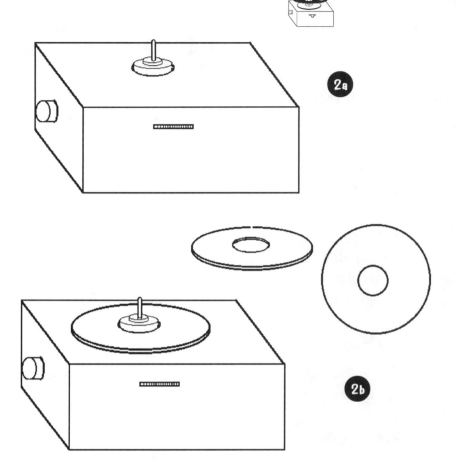

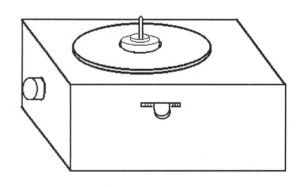

Step 3

Insert the Popsicle or craft stick into the slits (see diagram 3). The stick will hold the motor in place. If your box is too wide for one craft stick, overlap the tips of two sticks at least 2 inches and glue them together.

Step 4

Drill a hole or **hammer** a nail through the center of a block of wood. The hole should be slightly narrower than the diameter of the motor's spindle so it fits snugly into the hole. **Push** the spindle into the block of wood (see diagram 4a). **Set** the motor back into the box with the block of wood up (see diagram 4b). Experiment with different types of wood. Humidity levels will affect how well the wood stays on the spindle.

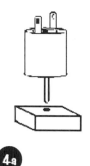

4a

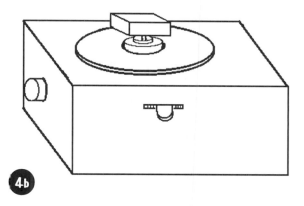

4b

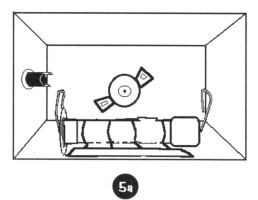

Step 5

Turn the box over. **Remove** the Popsicle or craft stick. **Tape** the battery pack in just above the slit on one side (see diagram 5a). Do not overtape; you will need to take the battery pack out to put in new batteries from time to time. **Reinsert** the craft stick (see diagram 5b). The stick will help to hold up the battery pack.

5a

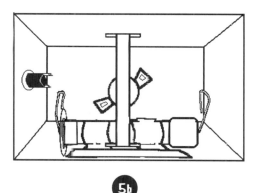

5b

Step 6

Measure the distances between the battery pack and the switch, the switch and the motor, and the motor and the battery pack. **Add** at least 2 inches to each measurement. **Cut** one piece of 22-gauge coated electrical wire for each measurement. With the wire stripper, **strip** the ends of each wire ¾ to 1 inch at each end.

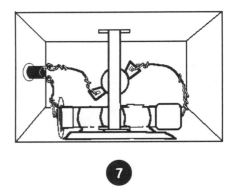

Step 7

Tightly **twist** together one stripped end of the battery pack-to-switch wire with the wire extending from the cardboard circle of the battery pack. **Insert** the other stripped end into the hole on one prong of the switch; **twist** tightly (see diagram 7). Tightly **twist** together one stripped end of the battery pack-to-motor wire with the wire extending from the plastic cap on the battery pack. **Insert** the other stripped end through the hole on one prong of the motor (see diagram 7). **Insert** one stripped end of the remaining wire through the hole on the other prong on the switch. **Twist** tightly. Then **insert** the other end through the hole on the other prong of the motor (see diagram 7). **Twist** tightly.

Step 8

Securely **tape** down all covered wires (see diagram 8). Be careful that the stripped wires do not touch.

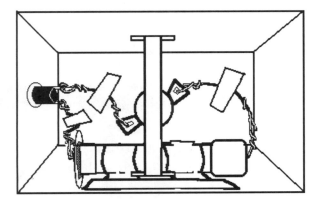

It is best to stick the wire through the hole in the post on the switch and motor, wrap the wire around the post, then twist it together (see diagram a). However, younger children may find it easier to slip it through the hole in the post, then twist it tightly together (see diagram b).

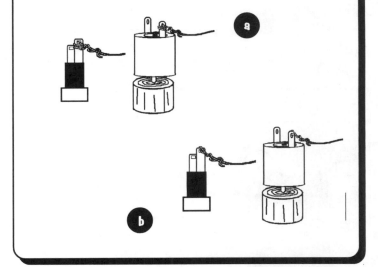

Step 9

Turn the box over; **push** the switch on and off to make sure the motor hums and the spindle spins. If they don't, check that your batteries are in correctly and that the wires are attached correctly.

90

ASSEMBLY

INSTRUCTIONS

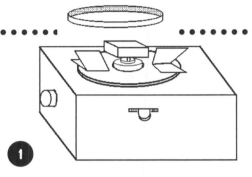

Step 1

Cut two 3-by-1½-inch pieces from the egg carton polystyrene or thick cardboard. **Fold** them in half lengthwise for the brakes. **Glue** one side of the brakes to the top of the box away from the block of wood, but close enough for the plastic lid or cardboard to cover them when it is centered on the block of wood (see diagram 1)

1

2

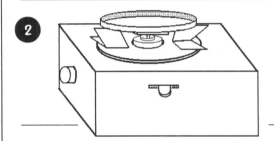

Glue the plastic lid, lip up, or cardboard circle to the block of wood, matching the centers (see diagram 2). **Push** the switch on to make sure that the brakes cause enough friction against the lid to slow the motor down.

Step 2

Step 3

Glue the bottom circle of the merry-go-round into the lid or onto the cardboard circle. Your merry-go-round is complete (see diagram 3).

3

SCIENCE EXPERIMENT

- Try thicker cardboard or polystyrene for the brakes. Test to see which thicknesses work best.

- Experiment with cutting your paper-plate circles less than 6 inches in diameter. Experiment with various diameters of circles to see which work best.

MOUSE

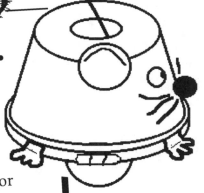 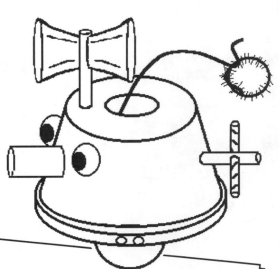

SUPPLIES

- one thick-tipped marker
- one good, strong (not brittle) 16-ounce plastic container, such as a medium sour cream or cottage cheese container
- one large piece heavy corrugated cardboard or mat board
- low-temperature mini-glue sticks
- one toilet paper tube
- cereal box or other lightweight cardboard
- two pipe cleaners
- two size 18 rubber bands
- one Popsicle or craft stick
- masking tape
- kite string 3 to 4 feet long
- paint
- construction paper and cardboard for features

TOOLS

- high-quality adult craft scissors with a spring in the handle
- ruler or compass
- low-temperature mini-glue gun
- hole punch
- heavy-duty cutting pliers
- paintbrush

INSTRUCTIONS

Step 1 With the thick-tipped marker, **trace** the bottom of the plastic container onto the thick cardboard (see diagram 1). You trace with the thick marker to make the circle slightly larger than the bottom. The diameter of the circle from outside of marker line to outside of marker line should be about 3³/₄ inches.

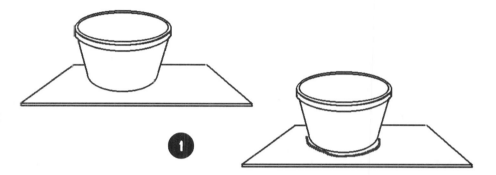

Cut along the outside of the marker line with the craft scissors (see diagram 2). **Step 2**

Step 3

Measure and **cut** a 1¹/₂- to 2-inch circle in the center of the cardboard (see diagram 3).

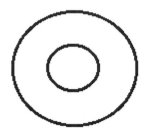

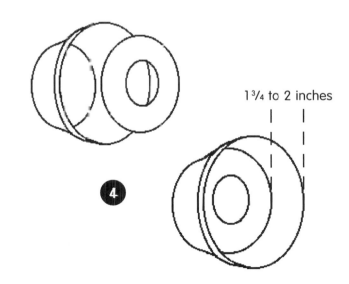

1³/₄ to 2 inches

Step 4

Insert the circle into the plastic container. It should fit snugly about 1³/₄ to 2 inches from the top of the lid (see diagram 4). If it is too big to fit that far in, trim small strips off the outside until it fits. Take the circle out and set it aside.

93

Step 5

Measure and cut a 1-inch-diameter hole in the center of the bottom of the plastic container (see diagram 5). To seal and smooth the edges, squeeze low-temperature glue around the rim of the hole in the plastic container.

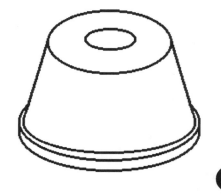

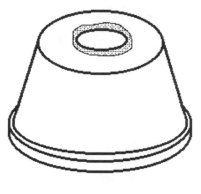

5

Step 6

Push the circle back into the container, and then **spread** low-temperature glue around the outside rim of the cardboard circle (see diagram 6). The glue and the cardboard will give the plastic container structural strength, which means the container will hold its shape under pressure. The mouse will need structural strength when you attach the rubber bands.

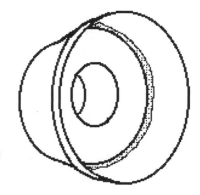

6

Step 7

With the hole punch, **punch** two holes close to the rim (into the lip of the container, if it has one) about ¼ inch apart into one side of the container (see diagram 7). **Punch** two more holes close to the rim directly across from the first two (four holes altogether). Be sure not to punch them too far up or the wheel will not have enough room to spin.

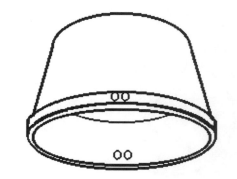

7

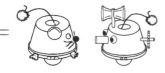

 **Step 8**

Cut a 3-inch or shorter piece from the toilet paper tube (see diagram 8a). **Insert** the piece horizontally into the container to make sure it fits with room to spare on either side (see diagram 8b).

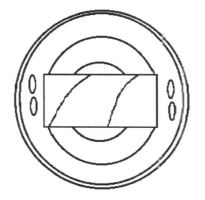

 **Step 9**

Trace an end of the toilet paper tube onto the cereal box cardboard twice (see diagram 9a). **Cut** out the two circles along the outer edge of the tracing. **Punch** a pair of holes into each one to match the pairs of holes you punched into the container (see diagram 9b).

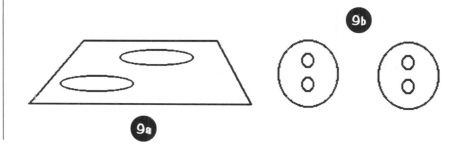

 **Step 10**

Use a low-temperature glue gun to **glue** one circle to one end of the piece of toilet paper tube (see diagram 10). Make sure the circle is really round and slightly larger than the end of the tube. If the circles are too small, then the wheel will not stay together. After the glue dries, look at the end closely to make sure the circle is securely attached all the way around. You may need to add more glue. It is not necessary to line up the holes in the two circles. **Attach** the second circle to the other end of the toilet paper tube in the same way.

   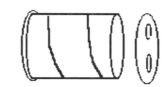 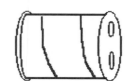

Insert one pipe cleaner through one rubber band. **Twist** the pipe cleaner to hold the band securely (see diagram 11a and page 29, step 12). **Repeat** with the other rubber band and another pipe cleaner. Carefully **thread** each pipe cleaner through one pair of opposite holes in the cardboard tube (see diagram 11b). If the holes on one end do not line up exactly with the holes on the other end, you can still get the pipe cleaners through the tube. Just stick the pipe cleaner into one side and watch it come out on the other side. Do not pull the pipe cleaners all the way through (see diagram 11c).

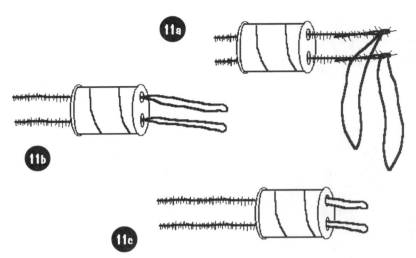

With the heavy-duty pliers, **cut** the Popsicle stick or craft stick in half crosswise (see diagram 12).

Insert the tube horizontally into the container, lining up the holes (the tube will extend about halfway out of the bottom of the container). **Push** the two pipe cleaners through the two holes on one side of the plastic container (see diagram 13). **Insert** the two rubber bands through the other two holes on the opposite side of the container (see diagram 13).

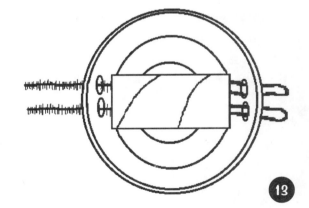

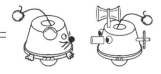

Step 14

Cut a strip or two of masking tape and **attach** them to your worktable to have them ready. **Insert** one stick half through the loops on the rubber bands (see diagram 14). Lightly tape the stick to the outside of the container just to hold it steady while you complete the next step.

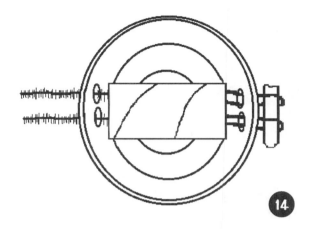

14

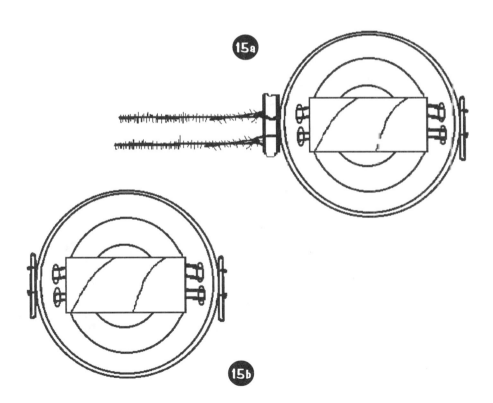

15a

15b

Step 15

Pull the pipe cleaners the rest of the way through the tube until the rubber bands are stretched far enough outside of the plastic container to put the other stick through them (see diagram 15a). **Remove** the tape and pipe cleaners from the other side of the container (see diagram 15b).

Step 16

Wrap the end of the kite string around the toilet paper tube one time and tie it securely with a small but secure knot (see diagrams 16a and 16b). The rest of the string should be hanging loose from the tube. **Apply** low-temperature glue to the knot and along the string where it touches the tube (see diagram 16b). Do not glob on too much glue. Any glue lumps may cause the wheel to hit against the cardboard circle and not turn.

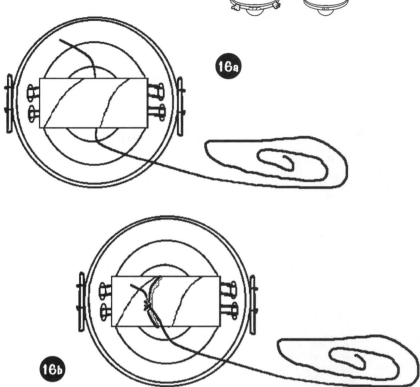

16a

16b

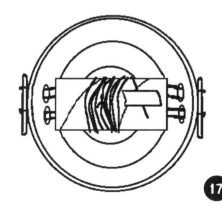

17

Step 17

Wrap the rest of the string around the toilet paper tube by turning the tube, winding the rubber bands. **Tape** the end of the string to the tube (see diagram 17). **Let go** of the wound-up tube to unwind the rubber bands.

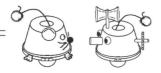

Step 18

Make a loop out of one of the pipe cleaners. **Twist** the ends together securely (see diagram 18a). **Remove** the tape from the end of the string. **Thread** the end of the string through the pipe cleaner loop and **knot** it securely around the pipe cleaner (see diagram 18b). **Squish** your pipe cleaner circle small enough to **push** it up through the hole in the cardboard above the tube, then through the hole in the bottom of the container. As you push the pipe cleaner through, the rubber bands will wind slightly, which will cause the string to pop back in place when you play with the mouse. **Pull** on the edges of your pipe cleaner loop to make it a circle again; otherwise, it will go back through the holes.

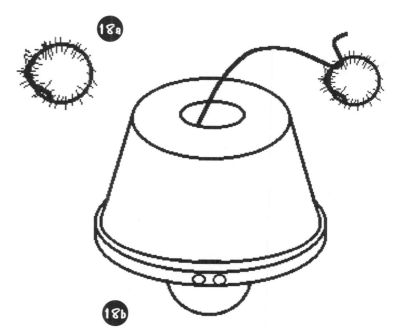

18a

18b

19

Step 19

Gently **pull** the string all the way out until it stops. Holding the string out, **set** the container on the floor, **let go** of the string, and **watch** it scurry away. **Mark** the front. **Paint** your creature. Use construction paper and cardboard scraps to **add** features—eyes, nose, whiskers, ears, feet, tail (see diagram 19).

TROUBLESHOOTING

- If the wheel is turning but the container is not moving, add some weight. You can add more or heavier decorations, but be careful not to overdo. Also, be sure to decorate it so the weight is distributed evenly.

- If the wheel does not turn, it is hitting against something. You may have used too much glue on the wheel or cut the wheel too long, or the cardboard ends covering the tube may not be round enough. Determine what is causing the problem. Unwind the string and make the necessary adjustments.

ADDITIONAL CREATURES

You can also make a cat, dog, space vehicle—whatever captures your imagination.

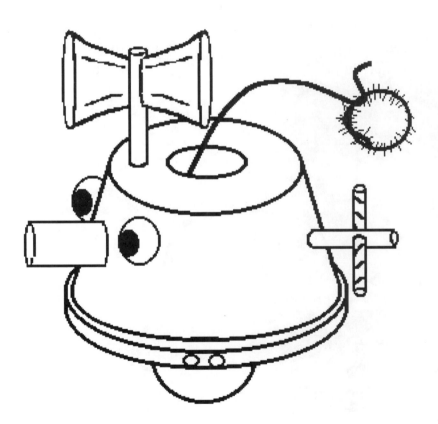

MOUSE

PARACHUTE

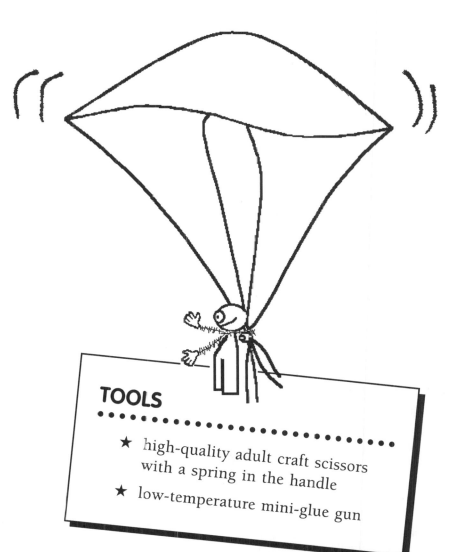

SUPPLIES
. . . .

+ one plastic grocery bag

+ yarn or string

+ masking tape

+ one clothespin or something of similar weight, such as a plastic vitamin pill bottle, plastic glitter bottle, or small juice container to use as person

+ paint

+ marker

+ decorations for the person

+ low-temperature mini-glue sticks

+ pipe cleaner

TOOLS
. . . .

★ high-quality adult craft scissors with a spring in the handle

★ low-temperature mini-glue gun

INSTRUCTIONS

Step 1

Cut the plastic grocery bag along the sides and across the bottom (see diagram 1).

1

Step 2

Find the center of one half, not counting the handles (see diagram 2).

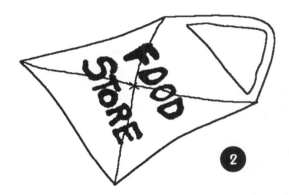

2

Step 3

Pinch the middle with your thumb and fingers and **smooth** the plastic down (see diagram 3).

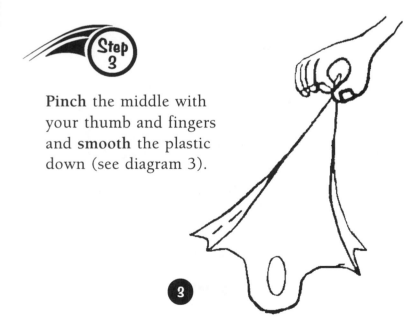

3

Step 4

Double-check your folds (the edges of the bag should be even) to make sure that you are holding onto the center of the plastic. **Squeeze** the handle end together, then **cut** straight across (see diagram 4).

4

Step 5

Open and **spread** out the piece you have remaining. It should be a perfectly round circle (see diagram 5).

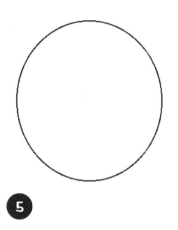

5

Step 6

Cut four 12-inch sections of thick string or yarn.

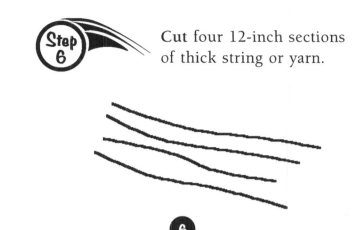

6

Step 7

Tape the strings to four equidistant points on the edge of the circle (see diagram 7). Be sure to **press** the tape securely down so that none of the sticky side of the tape is exposed. Otherwise, the tape will catch the edges of the parachute and it will not open.

Step 8

Tie the free ends of the four strings into a knot (see diagram 8).

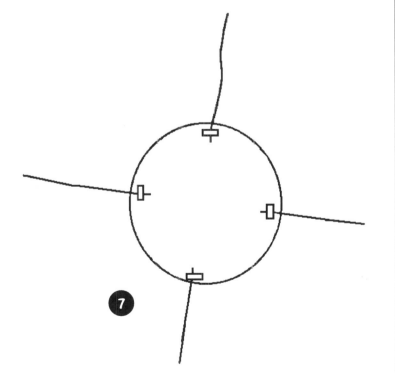

7

8

Step 9

Paint, **add features**, and **decorate** the item you will use as a person.

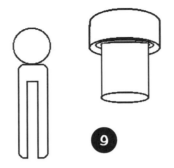

Step 10

With a pipe cleaner, **tie** your person securely to the knot in the parachute. You may want to **twist** the pipe cleaner so the ends come out in front like arms (see diagram 10). Add hands if you want.

TROUBLESHOOTING

If your parachute doesn't open, check your strings to make sure they are not tangled. If they aren't, throw it higher into the air to give it more time to open.

Step 11

Pinch the center of the circle and smooth the edges to close the parachute. **Fold** it up so you can throw it into the air. Do not wrap the string around the parachute. **Throw** it into the air and watch it float down.

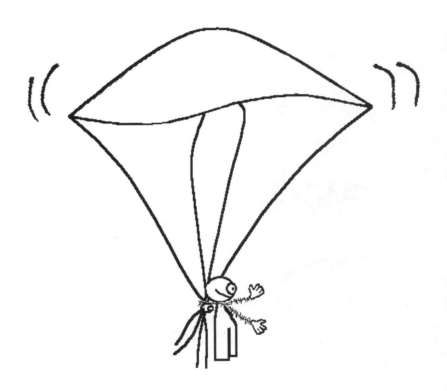

Experiment with various sizes of people and parachutes.

HYDRO ROCKET

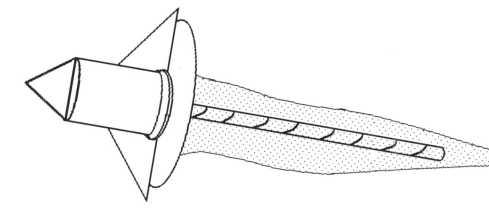

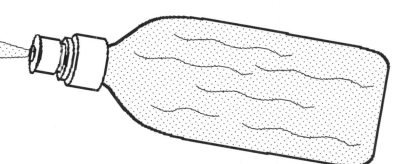

SUPPLIES

- ✦ one plastic sport water bottle
- ✦ one plastic lid
- ✦ low-temperature mini-glue sticks
- ✦ one plastic drinking straw
- ✦ one pill bottle or other small plastic container
- ✦ scraps of plastic for adding features to rocket

TOOLS

- ★ pliers
- ★ high-quality adult craft scissors with a spring in the handle
- ★ ruler
- ★ low-temperature mini-glue gun

INSTRUCTIONS

Step 1

With the pliers, **pull** the cap off of the water bottle top (see diagram 1a). **Snip** off the little plug so it will not block your straw later (see diagram 1b). **Replace** the sports cap (see diagram 1c).

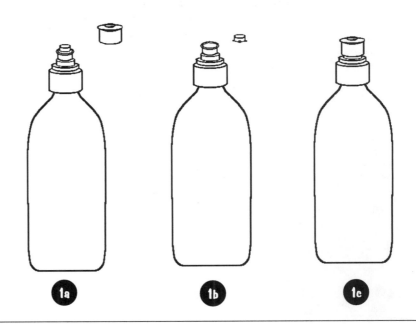

1a **1b** **1c**

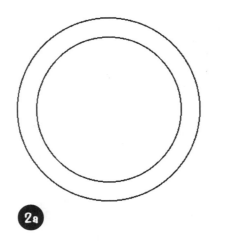

2a

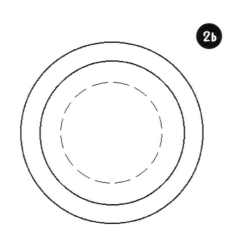

2b

Step 2

Draw a 1- to 2-inch diameter circle on a plastic lid (see diagram 2a). The circle has to be a little larger than the diameter of the pill bottle (see diagram 2b).

Step 3

Use the low-temperature glue gun to **glue** the straw onto the very center of the bottom of the plastic lid (see diagrams 3a, 3b, and 3c).

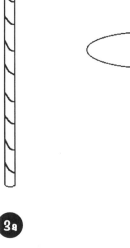

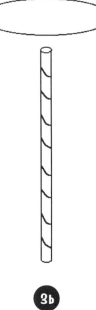

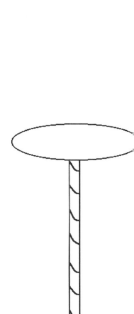

Step 4

Remove the lid from the small plastic container (see diagram 4a). **Turn** the bottle upside down (see diagram 4b) and **glue** it to the center of the plastic lid, opposite the plastic straw (see diagram 4c).

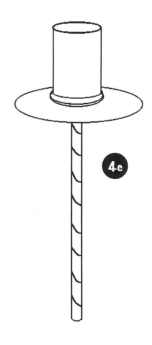

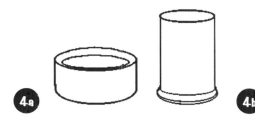

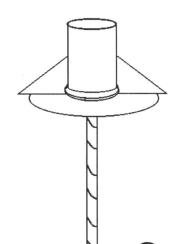

Step 5

Add plastic features to the bottle to make it look like a rocket (see diagram 5). The plastic makes it waterproof.

Step 6

Take the rocket outside. **Put** some water into the water bottle. **Push** the straw through the sports top and into the bottle, making sure the straw goes partway into the water (see diagram 6).

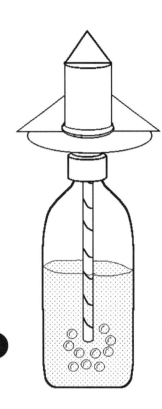

6

SCIENCE EXPERIMENT

- Use objects that are lighter and heavier than the pill bottle. Record how far each shoots. Speculate on your results.
- Different shapes shoot differently. Use various objects that are not rocket shaped. Record how far each shoots. Speculate.
- Don't put water in the bottle when you shoot the rocket. Do the objects fly better or worse when air is the force instead of water?

Step 7

Point the rocket into the air and squeeze the bottle strongly (see diagram 7). The rocket will shoot up into the air.

Warning

Do not aim the rocket at anyone.

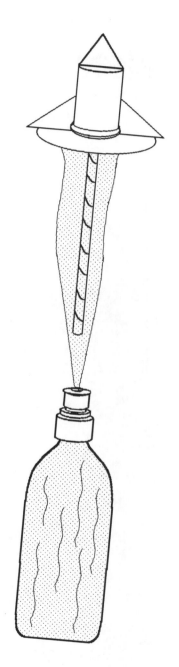

7

SUBMARINE

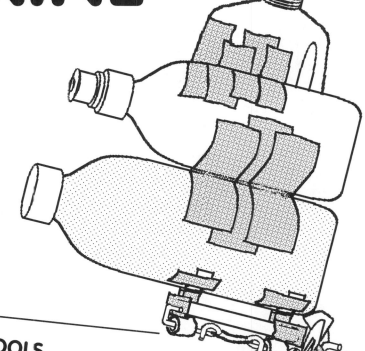

SUPPLIES

- ✦ duct tape
- ✦ two plastic 2- or 1-liter, or 12-ounce water, juice, or soda bottles that look like a submarine
- ✦ one plastic jug such as a milk jug for submarine decorations and the propeller bearing bracket
- ✦ four large beads with a hole large enough for a paper clip to go through
- ✦ one Popsicle or craft stick
- ✦ one large steel paper clip
- ✦ one 3- to 5-inch plastic lid, such as a margarine tub lid
- ✦ one 3-inch or smaller plastic lid, such as a yogurt container lid
- ✦ low-temperature mini-glue sticks
- ✦ two size 32 or 33 rubber bands
- ✦ dirt

TOOLS

- ★ heavy-duty diagonal cutters to cut paper clip
- ★ high-quality adult craft scissors with a spring in the handle
- ★ ruler
- ★ needle-nose pliers
- ★ low-temperature mini-glue gun

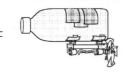

INSTRUCTIONS

 **Step 1**

Duct-tape the two plastic bottles together facing the same way (see diagram 1).

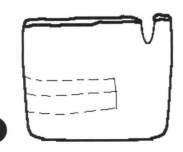

1

2a

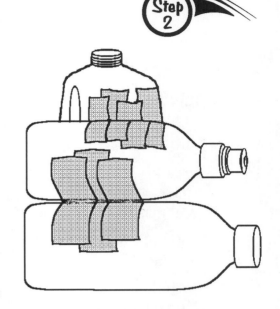 **Step 2**

Cut the top off the plastic jug (see diagram 2a). Duct-tape it perpendicular to the two plastic bottles (see diagram 2b).

2b

 **Step 3**

Cut two 1-by-8- to 10-inch strips of plastic from the bottom half of the jug.

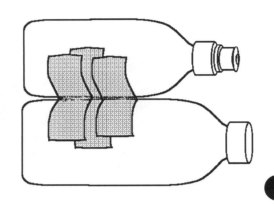

3

 **Step 4**

Glue a bead, hole facing out, into the center of each plastic strip (see diagrams 4a and 4b). Duct-tape the strips just above the bead (see diagram 4c), leaving the ends of the strips untaped (see diagram 4d). These are your propeller casings.

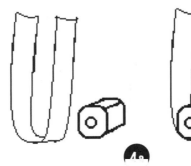

4a

4b

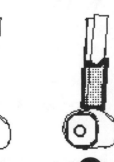

4c

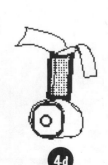

4d

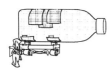

Step 5

Duct-tape one propeller casing to the bottom of the bottle, right near the back edge (see diagram 5). Duct-tape the second propeller casing slightly less than one craft stick length away.

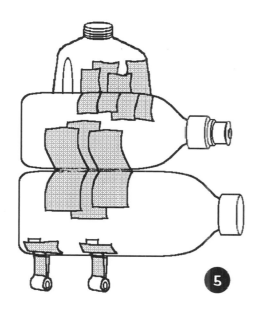

5

Step 6

Duct-tape the ends of the craft stick to the plastic strips (see diagram 6).

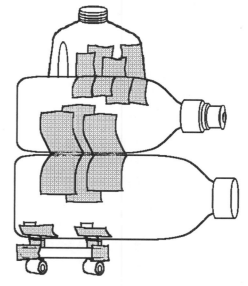

6

Step 7

Roll open the paper clip (see diagram 7a). Cut the clip into two pieces, with one piece being about ½ inch longer than the other (see diagram 7b).

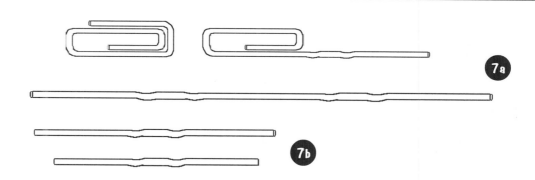

7a

7b

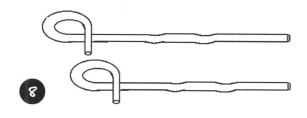

8

Step 8

With the needle-nose pliers, twist a loop into one end of each paper clip piece (see diagram 8).

needle-nose pliers

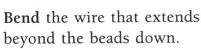

Step 9

Insert the longer clip into the hole in the back propeller casing with the loop facing the other casing (see diagram 9). **Place** two beads onto the extension behind the casing. **Insert** the shorter clip into the hole in the front propeller casing with the loop facing the other loop (see diagram 9).

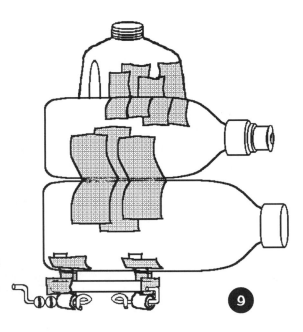

⑨

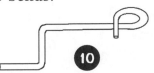

Step 10

Bend the wire that extends beyond the beads down. **Bend** it back about halfway down the extension (see diagram 10). Note that the diagram shows the length of the paper clip as if it were not in the casing so you can see how to bend it. It will still be inserted into the casing when you make the bends.

⑩

Step 11

On the front paper clip, **bend** the extension up where it emerges from the casing (see diagram 11). **Bend** it in about halfway between that bend and the end. **Bend** it down about halfway between the second bend and the end (see diagram 11).

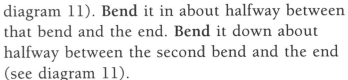

⑪

Step 12

Cut the larger plastic lid in half, then cut those pieces in half; you have quarters (see diagram 12a). **Cut** two pairs of slits directly across from each other in the smaller lid (see diagram 12b).

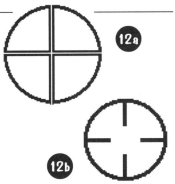

⑫ₐ

⑫ᵦ

Step 13

Insert the pieces of the larger lid into the slits in the smaller lid according to whether you are left- or right-handed (see diagram 13). **Glue** them securely with the glue gun. **Punch** a hole into the middle of the propeller large enough for the paper clip to go through (see diagram 13).

⑬

right-handed propeller   left-handed propeller

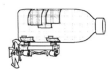

Step 14

Loop the rubber bands together. **Place** one end of the connected rubber bands onto each paper clip loop (see diagram 14). **Slide** the propeller onto the back paper clip. **Glue** the propeller in place, then firmly **duct-tape** it to the paper clip.

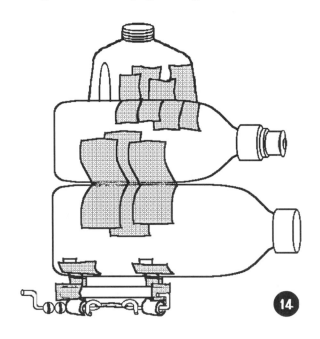

14

Step 15

Fill the bottom plastic container with dirt so it will submerge partway (see diagram 15). You may want to put water into the top one. **Place** the submarine in the water, **wind** up the propeller, and **let** it go.

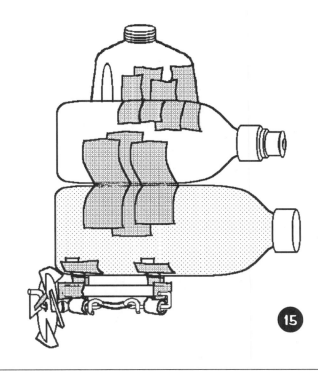

15

SCIENCE EXPERIMENT

- Put water into both bottles. What happens?
- Don't put anything in either bottle. What happens?
- Use various sizes and numbers of rubber bands. Large, loose-fitting rubber bands seem to work better with this propeller.

Glossary and Recommendations

acceleration: the rate of change of velocity; a body can accelerate by changing either its speed or direction

action and reaction: two forces that act whenever an object is moved; the moving force is the action, and the object resists or pushes back with a force called *reaction*

angle: the shape made when two straight lines meet at a point; the lever of the catapult as it touches the base

axle: the shaft that allows wheels to turn; the axle is a $\frac{1}{4}$-inch wooden dowel in the car and the pulley on the Ferris wheel

balance: the act of keeping an object level while suspended in the air by distributing weight equally on each end; equal weights on either side of a fulcrum

ball bearings: round beads that allow two objects to move easily, such as the fan and crank on the submarine

battery acid: cells that store energy as low-voltage electricity

brake: to slow the turning of a wheel by pushing an object against it to cause friction, such as on the merry-go-round

buoyant: able to float in water; aluminum can boats are buoyant

centrifugal force: moving away from the center of rotation of a spinning object

cereal box: lightweight, easy-to-cut, stiff, strong cardboard boxes; can also be found in shoeboxes, crayon boxes, and most boxes used to hold food products

corrugated cardboard: cardboard that has two layers of paper separated by a fan-shaped paper in the middle; easy to cut and strong enough for most projects; found in brown packing boxes used to ship canned goods; can cause problems because it easily bends and loses it shape

crank: a handle connected to a shaft that you turn or wind up to create movement

cutting: the act of using a sharp instrument to separate one piece of something into two; takes skill and practice. Take your time and get help when sawing wood, swimming pool noodles, and other materials

diameter: the width of a circle

dowels: round or square wooden sticks, usually 36 inches long, found in most hardware and craft stores; most projects work best with $\frac{1}{4}$-inch dowels, but if you have an accumulation of chop sticks from Asian restaurants, they work just as well if they are long enough; you can also adjust the project by making it smaller to fit the length of your chop stick

drag: the force with which air or water resists the motion of an object such as a car, boat, or aircraft; also called *water* or *air resistance*

drill: a little hand-crank craft drill works fine for the wood catapult when one or two people are building cars. The car requires a $1/32$ bit. But an electric drill operated by an adult is best for classroom projects that may require a lot of drilling. Never use a drill without adult supervision.

drilling: boring a hole into an object

drive belt: a belt that connects two pulleys to carry power from one pulley to the other; the drive belt for the Ferris wheel is made from rubber bands connected together into a large circle

duct tape: waterproof, very strong tape coated with aluminum. Don't use it on the electrical connections such as the car. Sticky and tangles easily. Don't wrap it around your fingers—it's tough to get off. The tape is easier to cut with adult-sized scissors that have not been abused. Don't use the same scissors you use to cut cardboard because cardboard makes the scissors dull over time. Use it only when you need to because it is difficult to work with. I usually put the cut end on the edge of a table and then pull a couple of feet out, holding the tape tight as I cut pieces I need.

electrical energy: energy supplied by continuous flow of electrons through a wire or other conductor

electrical tape: protective tape used to tape wires. After you finish wiring the car, wrap the bare wires with electrical tape. This tape is too stretchy to use to tape the motor down to the car (use masking tape for that), but it is great for covering the wires with a protective coating or taping the loose wires to the bottom of the car.

energy: the capacity to do work

foam core: polystyrene sandwiched between two sheets of paper; stiff and strong enough to use for the mechanical projects. It is easy to cut with an X-acto blade. Foam core is an excellent, structurally strong material to use as a base for any of the projects or the car frame. It may curl up slightly after painting.

force: the pushing and pulling of objects to cause them to move

friction: a force that occurs when one thing rubs against another, or when it moves through a liquid or gas

fulcrum: the point on which a lever is supported so that it can balance, swing, or tilt, such as the dowel on the catapult

glue: an adhesive used to hold two or more objects together. Use white wood glue for everything that the low-temperature hot glue is used for if you have time to let it dry; add white glue to tempera paint to make the projects stronger. Pour in equal amounts of glue and paint, then stir with your paintbrush. The multipurpose white glue can be used on paper, wood, cloth, and more.

glue gun: an electrical device shaped like a gun that heats up sticks of glue. Squeeze the trigger to force glue out of the gun onto the project. The glue cools quickly. A mini low-temperature glue gun works best on these projects.

gravity: the force that pulls objects to Earth and causes them to have weight

hammer or rock: a hammer is great for pounding nails into objects, but with more than one person working on the same project, I like to keep some rocks for hammers. They should be about the size of a closed fist.

hole punch: use a well-made hole punch to put holes into the projects. Putting holes in plastic containers and cardboard or foam core may take the grip of an adult.

inertia: resistance of a moving object to a change in its speed or direction; the resistance of a stationary object to being moved

kinetic energy: energy created by movement, such as rushing water, wind, or by sound, light, heat, or electromagnetic waves

lever: a simple machine with a rigid bar that pivots at a fulcrum to make it easier to lift and move a load

masking tape: an easy-to-use tape, inexpensive, and comes in different widths. You can cut it with practically any scissors or tear with your fingers.

mass: a measure of an object's inertia, that is, its heaviness; contrast with weight, which is a measure of gravitational force on an object

nail: when putting a nail hole through an object always put a board or thick cardboard under the object so that the nail does not go into your worktable. I use a nail instead of a drill or when a hole punch isn't strong enough.

paint: acrylic paint is excellent to work with, will stick to all the surfaces of the projects, but it doesn't wash out of clothes. Tempera paint only sticks to paper products that do not have a gloss coating, and it can stain your clothes. To use tempera mix glue into it. For structural strength pour in an equal amount of tempera paint and the white, multipurpose glue that says it works on paper, wood, cloth, pottery, and more. The glue dries almost clear so it doesn't change the color of the paint much. If I want a nice plastic, glossy look, then I pour in the thick, gooey tacky glue. It is a little harder to paint with but gives a nice finish.

paper tubes: sometimes you will need a thin paper tube and sometimes you will need a thicker one, but you shouldn't ever need the ones that are so thick that you can't use a hole punch on them. (You should be saving them for your projects).

pivot: the turning motion of the lever on the fulcrum.

pliers: a hand tool used for grasping that operates on a pivot using a lever/fulcrum principal. Needle-nose pliers have a tapered jaw with teeth and a cutting blade at the pivot. Heavy-duty diagonal cutting pliers are no larger than adult scissors but have a cutting edge that can cut heavy-gauge wire and 1/4-inch dowels.

polystyrene: a semi-hard, usually white foam used in shipping and packing. It is easy to saw, cut and poke, depending on its thickness. (Do not use the snowballs found in art and crafts stores for the cannon. If you can't find a good polystyrene ball then figure out a different object like the rectangular piece of cardboard shown in the cannon project.)

poster board: a cardboard about the same thickness as cereal boxes. Most poster board is too thin to work as a base.

potential energy: energy that is stored, such as in chemicals, fuels, and food

projectile: the object that flies or is thrust through the air

propeller: a device on the boat or submarine that thrusts the boat forward

pulley: a wheel that holds the drive belt, usually a groove cut into it to hold the belt on

range: the distance the projectile flies through the air

resistance: a force that slows the movement of an object; see also *drag*

rubber bands: the only sizes of rubber bands used in this book are 16, 18, 32, and 33. If you have a box of miscellaneous rubber bands and don't know their sizes, you can measure them: a size 16 is $2\frac{1}{2}$ inches by $\frac{1}{16}$ inch, an 18 is 3 inches by $\frac{1}{16}$ inch, a 32 is 3 inches by $\frac{1}{8}$ inch, and a 33 is $3\frac{1}{2}$ inches by $\frac{1}{8}$ inch.

rudder: a movable piece on the back of an airplane or boat.

safety: always the most important part of building your project. To avoid mishaps read the instructions and plan what you are going to do before your get started. Always have an adult present to help you.

scissors: adult scissors are the best to use for the projects. Use spring-loaded scissors to cut cardboard. I can't say enough good things about the springy scissors — they save a lot of work for your hands. I have a pair of heavy-duty diagonal-cutting pliers that I use to cut $\frac{1}{4}$-inch dowels and craft sticks. I also have a small pair of tin snips, which are perfect for cutting heavy cardboard. The pair I use has sharp, pointy tips and is good for making holes in things that a hole punch will not work on. Spring-loaded adult scissors are easier to use to cut all the different kinds of cardboard.

sewing: inserting string through a hole by means of a stronger, more rigid implement, such as a pipe cleaner or a sewing needle

shaft: a wooden stick that allows the wheels to turn and the Ferris wheel to spin

speed: the rate at which something moves

tension: the degree of tightness of something, usually rubber bands in this book

thrust: a sudden forceful push that propels something forward

velocity: speed in a particular direction

weight: a measure of gravitational force on an object

wheel and axle: a class of rotating machines or devices in which effort applied to one part produces a useful movement in another part

wheels: a disc that turns on a shaft or axle; may be used as a pulley on the Ferris wheel or the tires on the car.

About the Author

Carol McBride teaches arts and crafts, animation, cartooning, sleuthing, and carnival games to children ages 5 through 13. Her enthusiastic creativity inspires the same in the children she teaches. She has worked for the City of Tucson Parks and Recreation for five years, developing her own projects to suit individual classes.

Photo by Cassie McBride Gonzales

Machines on Back Cover

a. Propeller boat
b. Ferris wheel
c. Merry-go-round
d. Mouse
e. Catapult
f. Three-wheeled motor car

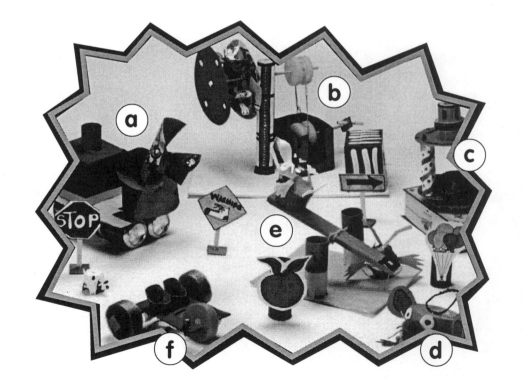

Create a Classroom of Excitement and Discovery with These Resources

DISCOVERING THE NATURALIST INTELLIGENCE
Science in the School Yard
by Jenna Glock, M.Ed., Susan Wertz, M.A., and Maggie Meyer, M.A.
foreword by Thomas R. Hoerr, Ph.D.
Grades 1–6

Apply this fresh approach to your curriculum and watch students come alive! All activities can be completed after a focused excursion into the average school yard or playground. By popular demand, here is the tool you need to help you—

- Define what the naturalist intelligence is and can achieve
- Identify naturalist traits in your students with an observational checklist
- Meet national science standards while using MI techniques in every lesson
- Strengthen your students' use of the naturalist intelligence with more than 30 outdoor lessons

1095-W . . . $29

Buy it on the web at http://www.zephyrpress.com/cgi-bin/zephyrcat/1095.html

SING A SONG OF SCIENCE
by Kathleen Carroll, M.Ed.
Grades K–6
featuring Gwendolyn Jenifer and the students of the Duke Ellington School of the Arts

You'll find that these classroom-tested songs, raps, and stories covering 16 topics are indispensable tools to reinforce science concepts you're already teaching. Explore these new dimensions in learning—

- Stories—the George Washington Carver story
- Raps—tropical rain forest rap, energy rap

- Songs—matter song, classifying song
- Resources—brain-based teaching overview, annotated references, web connections, and musical scores

35-minute audiotape and 64-page activity manual

1094-W . . . $27

Buy it on the web at http://www.zephyrpress.com/cgi-bin/zephyrcat/1094.html

Students love to make videos to show what they are learning

KIDVID
Fun-damentals of Video Instruction
by Kaye Black, M.Ed., NBCT
Grades 4–12

This comprehensive guide will help your students—

- Learn the basics of video production
- Develop analytical skills
- Construct criteria for evaluating video production
- Pay attention
- Demonstrate knowledge
- Utilize creative-thinking and problem-solving skills

Students learn about preproduction planning (scripting, etc.) and production techniques (camera work, lighting, etc.), then move into hands-on experience with the equipment.

1013-W . . . $25

Buy it on the web at http://www.zephyrpress.com/cgi-bin/zephyrcat/1013.htm

THREE CHEERS FOR TEACHING!
A Guide to Growing Professionally and Renewing Your Spirit
by Bonita DeAmicis

Staff Development

Become the teacher you know you can be with this simple yet transforming three-part professional growth plan. Exercises and activities show you how to turn ideas and dreams into actions and results. You'll have—

- 16 activities for discovering your uniqueness
- 7 ways you can gain knowledge to help you in the classroom
- 6 activities to help you examine your beliefs and values
- 8 ways to reinforce or acquire the 4 essential habits of a teacher

1098-W . . . $27.00

Buy it on the web at http://zephyrpress.com/cgi-bin/zephyrcat/1098.html

Discover how small changes in your teaching can reap big rewards in learning

BEGIN WITH THE BRAIN
Orchestrating the Learner-Centered Classroom
by Martha Kaufeldt, M.A.

Grades K–6

This book is for you if you want to—

- Apply brain research to your classroom but aren't sure how
- Attempt to control chaos in your classroom
- Create systems and strategies with the brain in mind

Here's an example of what you'll find—

- Questions to ask yourself when designing classroom procedures
- 6 ways to categorize classroom routines, from reading circles to completing math tasks
- 12 ways to build positive awareness of ourselves and our peers
- 4 ways to inspire curiosity and minimize anxiety
- Dozens of ideas for meeting psychological needs of belonging, power, freedom, and fun

1102-W . . . $32

Buy it on the web at http://www.zephyrpress.com/cgi-bin/zephyrcat/1102.html

---

Shop online for more products and great specials!
http://www.zephyrpress.com

Qty.	Item #	Title	Unit Price	Total
	1095-W	Discovering the Naturalist Intelligence	$29	
	1094-W	Sing a Song of Science	$27	
	1013-W	KidVid	$25	
	1098-W	3 Cheers for Teaching	$27	
	1102-W	Begin with the Brain	$32	

Name _____

Address _____

City _____

State _____ Zip _____

Phone (_____) _____

E-mail _____

Subtotal	
Sales Tax (AZ residents, 5%)	
S & H (10% of subtotal–min $4.00)	
Total (U.S. funds only)	

CANADA: add 22% for S & H and G.S.T.

Method of payment (check one):

❑ Check or Money Order   ❑ Visa

❑ MasterCard   ❑ Purchase Order Attached

Credit Card No. _____

Expires _____

Signature _____

Please include your phone number in case we have questions about your order.

Call, Write, or FAX for your FREE Catalog!

Zephyr Press®

REACHING THEIR HIGHEST POTENTIAL

P.O. Box 66006-W
Tucson, AZ 85728-6006

1-800-232-2187
520-322-5090
FAX 520-323-9402